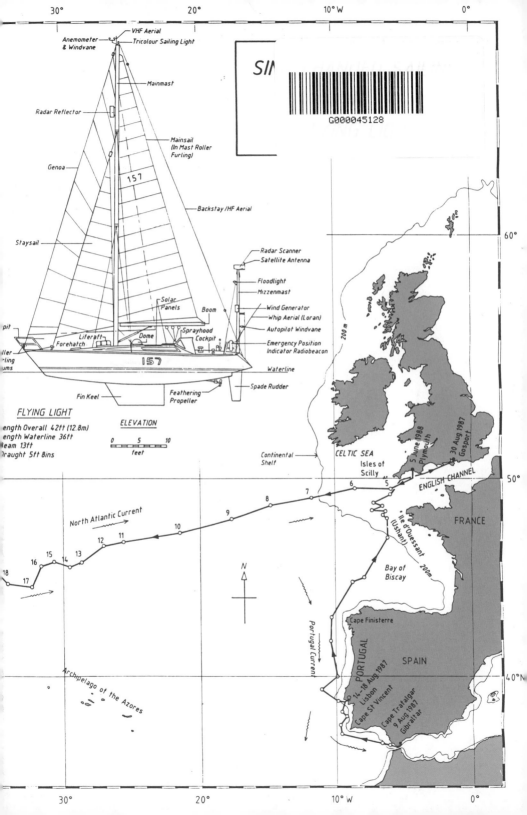

SIM

G000045128

Elevation labels (sailboat diagram):

- VHF Aerial
- Anemometer & Windvane
- Tricolour Sailing Light
- Mainmast
- Radar Reflector
- Mainsail (In Mast Roller Furling)
- Genoa
- Backstay / HF Aerial
- Staysail
- Radar Scanner
- Satellite Antenna
- Floodlight
- Mizzenmast
- Solar Panels
- Boom
- Wind Generator
- Whip Aerial (Loran)
- Autopilot Windvane
- Emergency Position Indicator Radiobeacon
- Literaft
- Forehatch
- Dome
- Sprayhood
- Cockpit
- Waterline
- Spade Rudder
- Fin Keel
- Feathering Propeller

pit
ller
-ling
ums

FLYING LIGHT

Length Overall 42ft (12.8m)
Length Waterline 36ft
Beam 13ft
Draught 5ft 8ins

ELEVATION

0   5   10
feet

Continental Shelf

Map labels:

- 200 m
- CELTIC SEA
- Isles of Scilly
- 5 June 1988 Plymouth
- 30 Aug 1987 Gosport
- ENGLISH CHANNEL
- FRANCE
- Île d'Ouessant (Ushant)
- Bay of Biscay
- 200 m
- North Atlantic Current
- Portugal Current
- N
- Cape Finisterre
- PORTUGAL
- SPAIN
- 14 – 18 Aug 1987 Lisbon
- Cape St Vincent
- Cape Trafalgar 9 Aug 1987 Gibraltar
- Archipelago of the Azores

Map numbers along route: 5, 6, 7, 8, 9, 10, 11, 12, 13, 14, 15, 16, 17, 18

Coordinates: 30°, 20°, 10° W, 0°, 60°, 50°, 40° N

In at the Deep End

IN AT THE DEEP END

Denise St. Aubyn Hubbard

JANUS PUBLISHING COMPANY
London, England

First published in Great Britain 1993 by
Janus Publishing Company

Copyright © Denise St. Aubyn Hubbard 1992

British Library Cataloguing in Publication Data
Hubbard, St. Denise Aubyn
  In at the Deep End
  I. Title
  797.092

  ISBN 1-85756-031-0

Phototypeset by Intype, London

Printed and bound in England by
Antony Rowe Ltd, Chippenham, Wiltshire

FOR JOHN
whose friendship, seamanship and generosity
of spirit have been my inspiration

Contents

Qualified to Command

'Starboard twenty, slow ahead port, slow astern starboard.'

The forward spring was still secured to help cant out the stern.

'Stop both engines, let go spring, midships, slow astern both engines.'

Portisham's powerful diesels thrust her away from the constricted berth in Vernon Creek. I turned and headed for Fareham Creek to demonstrate ship handling alongside the disused naval vessels moored there: all part of my examination for command of Royal Naval Auxiliary Service (RNXS) vessels, the only service then to accept women for sea. Skipper candidates had to qualify in ship handling, pilotage and coastal navigation for duty afloat. The examination was taking place at the naval shorebased establishment HMS *Vernon*, Portsmouth, and on board *Portisham*, a twin-screw, 108 foot Ham class ex-inshore minesweeper. Commander Farquharson, Area Naval Auxiliary Officer, was examining us.

I had left home in my sea rig to avoid changing on board, one less detail to think about. I had taken down the 0625 hours shipping forecast, sharpened my seaman's knife and cleaned the lanyard. I arrived on board and stowed my gear in an after cabin. Chartwork was the first examination. My mind went blank but as the subject took over I settled down and completed the paper in time, after which we had to prepare a passage and anchorage plan for our voyage next day.

After breakfast the ship was secured for sea and I found myself duty skipper for the first twenty-four hours. The mate reported crew were present and correct as the Admiralty gyro magnetic compass and radar were started and the echo sounder and loud hailer switched on. Wheel, telegraph and whistle were tested as well as visual signals including 'not under command' lights. Very pistol and cartridges were stored in the ready use position under the skipper's chair and the radio-telephone and VHF tuned to the required frequency and channel. The charge engineer reported engine readiness and fuel and fresh water supplies; anchors were ready for letting go and mooring lines singled up. Ten minutes before departure the two 350hp Paxman diesels roared into life. The communicator requested permission to slip from Queen's Harbour Master. I would take *Portisham* out stern first from the berth en route to Fareham Creek for manoeuvres called circuits and bumps, hopefully without any bumps!

That afternoon we went off for survival and liferaft drill in the swimming pool where examination nerves evaporated in the water; I had been in and out of swimming pools all my life. Later we made passage to Yarmouth Roads in the Solent where we secured to a mooring buoy, holding *Portisham* steady while the buoy jumper leaped on to the buoy, passed a warp through the ring and climbed back on board, enthusiastically assisted by the crew. The ship could then be heaved up to the buoy and a cable shackled to the buoy ring for greater security. The stronger the wind and tidal stream, particularly in wind against tide conditions, the more difficult it was to hold the ship alongside the buoy.

Our return to Vernon Creek was followed by two short night passages in and out of Portsmouth harbour. I had prepared a comprehensive passage plan including tracks, distances, leading lights, buoy names and light characteristics each in chronological order, as the numerous lit navigation buoys, lighthouses and bright shore lights could be confusing. By means of the voice pipe from bridge to charthouse, the navigator was informed as each buoy at the edge of the channel was identified and abeam. He then noted the time and the position reached in his log book and checked on the next course to steer. All went according to plan.

As duty navigator on the third day I prepared the passage plan and marked up the tidal stream atlas. Under way I was busy with chartwork, fixing position, projecting courses ahead and estimated times of arrival at various points for the skipper's information. Later that day I was on the wheel. *Portisham* had no power assisted steering: just a heavy wooden wheel with rudder indicator 0°–35° port and starboard. For me, 20° of wheel meant taking a step back to wind it round as fast as possible. Wheel and engine orders were repeated by the helmsman and the engineer on the bridge controls to confirm both had heard correctly; then when the orders had been executed, helmsman and engineer so reported. In this way there was no chance of misunderstanding: the skipper remained in command of the manoeuvre throughout.

For the afternoon passage I was duty mate in charge of the upper deck and responsible for the prompt and proper execution of the skipper's orders. I had to see that the warps were properly stowed after slipping and that before coming alongside they were correctly led, that heaving lines were coiled and anchors ready for letting go.

On day four the Captain RNXS was to ship aboard and we made sure the ship was spick and span for his visit. In the morning we practised anchoring in St Helen's Roads, Isle of

Wight. I had to select a place on the chart and anchor in that exact position. This was done by approaching on a transit from two shore marks while cross bearings on another mark abeam were checked repeatedly until the planned 'stop engines' bearing was reached. *Portisham* would then carry her way to the 'let go' bearing. The examiner was monitoring our progress on the radar. On my order to let go, the blake slip pin was knocked out and the anchor cable snubbed on the brake as necessary to control the speed of veer, the mate calling out the shackles (the length of cable run out) from the eye of the ship. A three point bearing recorded the ship's position and the time and depth from the echo sounder were noted. Tidal height was worked out and subtracted from the total depth of water to find the depth below chart datum to which was added the height of tide at high water. The depth of water at high tide thus predicted was then multiplied by three for short stay and by five for long stay at anchor to determine how much cable to veer.

Portisham had two 200lb anchors and antimagnetic cable with four and a half shackles (405 feet) on one anchor and six and a half shackles (585 feet) on the other. Each shackle of the bronze cable, fifteen fathoms long (each fathom measuring six feet), was marked with white paint and seizing wire. As there was no power on the windlass it was hard work weighing anchor, with one seaman on each windlass handle and other seamen waiting to take over in relays. The mate called out the shackles at the waterline and how the anchor cable grew; as the cable came home the engineers put pressure on the hoses for the seamen to scrub it free of mud with long handled brooms. When the anchor was brought home it was secured with brake, pawl and blake and screw slips.

On the fifth and final day crew and candidates cleaned ship. We candidates then sat a final examination paper on various subjects including tidal heights and how to pass a tow. When it was over I was called in to the Commander's office and told that I had passed and was now qualified to command this beautiful vessel. I went home to Bosham in a daze and for the next eight years found myself the only woman skipper in the RNXS.

2

Childhood

I was born in London on 19 February 1924, but my first memories were of a Cairo flat fairly high up. My parents, James and Jess Newman, my brother Derek (Del) and I arrived there in August 1925 when I was eighteen months old. After two and a half years we moved to the village of El Ma'adi, seven miles to the south. The eleven years there stand out clearly in my mind even today. I loved it. To my first school in Ma'adi, run by white-haired Miss Ray, I cycled the half mile myself, once proficient, since there was little traffic.

East of Ma'adi was the beautiful desert with the brown velvet Mokhattam hills in the distance. To the west ran the fast flowing Nile while to the north and south grew fields of *berseem* (tall clover for cattle), *doura* (maize), beans and sugar cane.

The houses were varied, designed by architects of different nationalities, and flowers and fruit grew in abundance in the fertile Nile soil. Eucalyptus, mauve-coloured jacaranda and glowing flame trees dominated the oleander bushes lining the streets. Bougainvillaea, morning glory and wisteria climbed our house and balcony. My parents took on extra land. This was turfed and planted by the gardener, Abouserih, to my mother's plans. He grew a profusion of flowers of all kinds, some of English stock including roses, hollyhocks, zinnias with their starched petticoats, antirrhinums, chrysanthemums, stocks, pansies, petunias, frangipani and violets.

Trellises of grapes hung over a large fishpond. The goldfish liked being tickled as they swam between the water lilies; when the sun went down the sound of frogs and crickets filled the air. There were orange trees and tangerines (called *Yussef Effendi*), apricots or *mish mish*, bananas, figs, dates, mangoes, guavas and cape gooseberries which were bright orange inside their paperlike covers. I could not keep my hands off the fruit, much to my mother's disgust when she needed grapes for the table only to find, as we tried each variety in turn, half eaten bunches under the paper wrappings used as a protection against the birds.

The house was spacious and airy with a verandah, large sitting room, dining room and a hall where all the tennis rackets and riding gear seemed to end up. There was a balcony and a large flat roof where we played a lot, climbing up on to the parapet and jumping off although this was forbidden as it was three floors up and it was feared we might stumble the wrong way. The house was full of children who always seemed to congregate at our place as a matter of course. They did not need an invitation but came to play endless games of ping-pong on the verandah, chess, tree climbing and romping with the animals.

Egyptians had a lean time, particularly the children and the animals, for the country was very poor. Whenever my mother saw a lame donkey, a horse covered in sores or stray dogs and cats with bones sticking out, she would rescue them with great gusto and my help too. Horses and donkeys either would go to the Shuffakhana run by the state, to be cured at a cost of five piastres a day (a shilling, unthinkably expensive for the poor), or with the owner's consent could go free to the hospital founded by Lady Brookes to rescue English horses left behind after the 1914-18 war and shamefully neglected.

Many emaciated cats and dogs ended up at our place soon to blossom after regular food and love. In our model T Ford car I usually ended up on the floor while the dogs occupied the back seat squabbling and barking excitedly when they sighted other animals.

Later we kept one of the rescued donkeys we had bought from the owner. Molly was both cross and lazy, kicking anyone so foolish as to pass behind, but whenever she went out with the horses my mother rode she would canter untiringly over the desert. Early each morning I crept downstairs to let out the dogs and lead Molly from her stable. I would pick out her feet, oil her hooves and groom her before careering down the road towards the desert with that ragged pack of hounds.

Too Too, a beloved and well-behaved greyhound, was white with large brown patches and nearly my age. She was most elegant, but if she decided to nip Arab cyclists in long *galabiehs* it was done so discreetly and innocently that no one could believe she was responsible. She was a good watchdog and had a deep bark on the very few occasions when she needed to speak. Darling Too Too, her nose was put out of joint as more and more strays were brought in.

Ma'adi had no street lights and few of the roads were macadamized. The little railway station lay about a mile from our house, between us and the Nile. When I was old enough to go to the English School in Cairo I travelled daily to Bab el Luk station to be picked up there by the school bus. The diesel trains bounced so much that Ahmed, the cook, who was elderly and went to Cairo once or twice a week to shop, was terrified we would be derailed.

The climate, hot and dry in summer and cold and dry in winter, suited me well. Rain bucketed down for two days a year, a great novelty, and the desert blossomed overnight. There were glorious sunsets, particularly in the desert, but no twilight; it was dark as soon as the sun went down when the frogs and crickets began their magical chorus.

Ma'adi's club had a swimming pool, tennis courts, cricket pitch and a golf course that led out into the desert. The pool was 33 ⅓ metres long with 1 metre and 3 metre springboards and a 5 metre firm board. The pool was drained each evening and scrubbed. We played while the water went out and the pool was then refilled with cold artesian well water from 500 feet down, disinfected with copper sulphate.

In the summer our house shutters were kept closed during the heat of the day except for the French windows on the verandah, as children and animals were always dashing in and out that way. White fishnet cotton curtains tried to keep out the flies, my good-natured father's pet hate. The curtains were a shambles since we put our hands straight through them to open the windows, easier than parting them, and the dogs entangled themselves as they attempted to clamber through.

Insects were not too bad: we rarely saw scorpions and the deadly sand viper was only glimpsed rarely in the desert. Flying ants I hated, especially in the mating season when they would flood out on the stairs and all over the bath. When I was about five years old there was a plague of locusts and the air was thick and dark with them. The children were offered piastres for catching them when the swarms were easily within our reach. Del did the catching while I did the picking up. I did not really want to but I knew they devastated the crops and so I followed the other children.

My father, who had two horses shot from under him in the 1914–18 war, was a good horseman, but in Egypt seldom found time to go out. My mother, who rode spirited Arab horses, taught me to ride. My instructions if I fell off were to hold on to the reins or we would have to chase the animals across the desert! Since they spent much time bucking and rearing I fell off constantly until my grip improved. They had a disconcerting habit of going straight from a walk to a gallop as soon as the reins were gathered up. One excitable Arab horse had to be blindfolded before he would even let me mount him. I certainly learned how to fall.

Despite a good appetite I was very skinny and except when immersed in a book or asleep, found staying still extremely difficult. No doubt all the home cooked food and six o'clock bedtime gave me this strength.

All our food was home-cooked and the gamoose (water buffalo milk), had to be boiled because of germs. It was rich milk which produced clotted cream when cold. Lemonade made from fresh limes was always available and a large ice chest kept things cool; ice was delivered every day.

Animal feeding time was twice a day and hectic. They were fed on fresh cooked meat and roughage and this was dished out in bowls in the garden. It was necessary to keep watch since the newly arrived animals could not get used to the fact that they would now have regular meals so they bolted their own food and then tried to eat everyone else's. At the same time the black crows made constant dives into any dish left unguarded for a moment. Ticks were a great scourge and these had to be removed every day from the dogs' coats and ears. It was a horrible job using tweezers and dropping them into tins of paraffin. These ticks swelled up very quickly and, if left unattended, the dogs ran the risk of getting tick fever.

On Christmas Day we usually went riding early before friends came round for drinks and lunch. There was liable to be a flood of tears when the turkey was served as we always fattened up two of them. They gobbled incessantly and occasionally found their way into the house, aided and abetted by me, and had unfortunately become my friends.

My parents sang in the chorus of various Gilbert and Sullivan operettas which were staged by amateurs and produced by a one-time professional in aid of charity at the Opera House, Cairo. The Opera House was internationally known. Built entirely of wood in three weeks I believe, by the Khedive Ismail in 1869 to celebrate the opening of the Suez Canal. It was to stage the opera Aida complete with elephants for the visit of the Empress Eugene. There was a rabbit warren of cellars where permanent staff made and maintained costumes to dress entirely almost any production. Well known artists from all over the world performed there including Pavlova. In 1971 I read in the papers that it had burnt down and that the general public and artists of all nationalities wept in the street to see the end of this marvellous building and all it stood for.

Both my parents had an excellent sense of humour. Daddy was very quiet with a dry wit, Mummy talkative with lots of restless energy. Self-taught, she loved painting and making things. I would get her to make up stories when she tucked me up at night; they became so outrageous that we grew hysterical with laughter till the tears poured down our faces. My own children became equally enchanted with her tales. Despite the laughter she was the family disciplinarian. As a child I picked up colloquial Arabic effortlessly from the servants, as children do, and could readily switch from one language to the other. I liked the Egyptians with their marvellous sense of humour and had friends of every nationality.

Most children could swim from an early age, and we learned much from water play as we grew older. One game, 'Pom Pom', had one person in the middle of the pool and about twenty or so on the side. We had to keep diving in and swimming across without being tapped on the back. This was easy to start with but those caught then joined the catcher in the pool. When all but one, usually me, had been caught, it was a different matter. Then you had to run the gauntlet of people waiting to pounce stretching down the whole length of the pool as you swam across. Best was to swim on your back touching the bottom and fight them off from rolling you over before you were across. This went on all morning sometimes, in and out and back and forth under water, your second wind coming without your knowing it.

Del went home to prep school when he was eleven and then on to public school. In those days there was no easy air travel, and children at school in England returned to Egypt only in the summer holidays by ship. There was great excitement for them in travelling to and fro, and so many parties were laid on when they arrived, but the thought of a whole year away I found horrific.

My mother loved the old quarter of the Mousky in Cairo where she would haggle in the little shops and stalls. Beautiful old houses with Moushrabeih carvings, the mosques of Ibn Tulun and Sultan Hassan dating from the Mameluke period and the Mohammed Ali mosque and the Citadel were a joy to behold. Driving in Cairo was hectic; cars raced at break-neck speed with a finger on the horn and a foot hovering on the brake to avoid the pedestrians and overloaded donkeys who swarmed over the roads. Our old car occasionally broke down, which meant sending for Tewfik, the house servant, who came post haste to right it. A natural mechanic, he much preferred cars to housework.

In the summer holidays my father would meet Del at Port Said. Outings to the pyramids at Giza and camel rides then followed. I climbed the great pyramid of Cheops, nearly 500 feet high, when I was fourteen. It took quite a time to reach the top from where there was a marvellous view over Cairo. Cheops had long since lost its limestone cladding, unlike nearby Chephren which still had some left near its peak preventing a full ascent.

Another interesting trip was to the caves of Masara between

Ma'adi and Helwan further south where the sulphur baths were. The stone to build the pyramids was cut from these hills and the gigantic blocks were floated down the Nile to Giza. The hills were honeycombed with caves, and we took balls of string, torches and magnesium wire to illuminate them and prevent us falling down some bottomless pit never to be seen again.

Every three years we went home by ship for three months' leave. I loved shipboard life and the games on board, always insisting, for no known reason, on being shown over the vast engine rooms. England was excitingly strange when it rained. Inevitably I would get into my bathing costume and run out into it and down to the beach if we were staying near the sea.

But we were always delighted to get back to Ma'adi.

3

In Training

Egypt

My mother taught me to dive. My style was pretty but technically incorrect. Ten dives a morning at weekends and in
school holidays while my friends were playing convinced me
I was hard done by. At the age of six I won my first cup for
diving and from then on a good many club competitions,
both swimming and diving for Ma'adi against Heliopolis,
Tewfikieh, Gezira and other clubs. In 1934 at the age of ten,
I gave a diving exhibition at Tewfikieh Tennis Club from the
3 metre springboard and 5 metre platform which first attracted
press attention.

In 1935 I won the junior Victor Ludorum athletics prize at
the English School in Cairo where I was a day girl, and again
in 1936 when I broke both the 100 and 200 yard records. At
Tewfikieh pool, Zamalek in October 1936, when I was twelve,
I broke the junior 50 metre freestyle record and equalled
the senior 50 metre time. *The Sphinx*, an English-language
magazine, described me as 'Heroine of the day, Denise
Newman, whose remarkable turn of speed clipped two
seconds off the record'. Ma'adi also won the relay race in

which I usually swam last leg. From then on I started to be noticed as a swimmer as well as a diver.

Although I never took athletics seriously, probably because I had no coach to push me and did no training, I won the senior school Victor Ludorum both in 1937 and 1938. In 1937 I was first in the Arab horse race on a beautiful borrowed mount at Mena House Gymkhana. I had not raced before and found it exhilarating.

That September, aged thirteen and accompanied by my mother, I went to Alexandria for the open Egyptian championships to give a diving display. I was persuaded to enter a couple of freestyle races for fun. Despite troublesome earache I broke the records for both the open 50 metre and 100 metres freestyle in the heats, semi-finals and finals against girls of eighteen to twenty-three. Ma'adi Club broke the relay record. My mother and I were presented to King Farouk, then a slim young man, who congratulated me and presented my medal. The press, ever kind and supportive, seemed to go wild, in particular the French newspaper *La Bourse Egyptienne*, which proclaimed 'Denise Newman FOR EVER, the big little champion'. They all made much of my dancing, athletics and riding as well. I suppose it made good copy then to have someone young and shy, who was versatile the year round.

Later that month, while I was diving at Mena House Hotel pool at Giza, I met Ahmed Ibrahim Kamel, an Egyptian architect known as Kelly. He had dived for Egypt in the 3 metre springboard event in the previous year at the Berlin Olympics, thought I had potential and offered to coach me. Little did my mother and I realise what we were in for! He decided I would enter for the open Egyptian diving championships then three weeks away. Since my technique was incorrect and I could perform none of the eight dives required for international competition, it seemed a hopeless venture.

There are five groups of dives: forward, backward, twisting, reverse and back front. Each has a tariff or degree of difficulty which is multiplied by the average marks to give a final total. The 3 metre springboard international compulsory dives in 1937 were: flying front somersault in the tucked position; back somersault in the straight position; reverse dive (or half gagnor) piked (ie. jackknife position); and back dive with half twist straight. My optional dives were: 1½ forward somersault piked; 1½ back somersault piked; reverse somersault tucked also known as full gagnor or molberg; back front (or cut away) 1½ somersault tucked. In those days women were not allowed to perform the more difficult dives in competitions.

Kelly was delightful: tall, quiet and strict but an excellent if difficult coach – as good ones usually are. He worked me intensively for three hours each morning and two in the afternoon. My mother thought it was a bit much but her protests were met with an icy 'Madam, you are here to educate and feed the child, I am her coach'.

In the middle of all this intensive training I caught dengue fever, a sort of virulent flu. Up to the last couple of days my marks were far below those of my rivals, and I was inconsistent where consistency counted. Timing is essential in diving. For example, in the 1½ back somersault tucked it was necessary to lift high and straight off the springboard, hips spinning, head tucked into my knees until I saw the end of the board when I shot my legs out straight towards it to check the spin, dropped my head back to look for the water, closed my arms above my head and stretched hard for entry.

Competition nerves handicapped me. Weak from stage fright, I could barely stand on the board without wobbling. This made consistent diving difficult but proved advantageous in swimming, when fear was the catalyst for high speed! In practice my poor times drove my coach demented, but I broke records on the day. I had no sense of urgency during training

17

when it was not for real, but always pulled out my best in the relay, usually as last leg. Kelly was a hard task master: dive after dive after dive. He gave me no idea of how I was getting on but was ever correcting and never praising. Eventually I learned that when pleased he would turn his back so that I could not see him smile.

16 October 1937 saw the start of the open Egyptian championships at Gezira. Suddenly I was on top form with virtually every dive. First I won the 3 metre springboard championship – unbelievable. Then I won the 5 metre platform diving the following day. Kelly was delighted, as were we all. His hard work had certainly paid off.

Early on in my training I had been asked to give an exhibition of springboard diving at this same Gezira pool during a gala. When my display was over, Kelly announced without consulting anyone, that I would now dive off the 10 metre platform (33 feet). I had never even been up there before, let alone dived off. It was a different technique and from that height you could afford no mistakes on entry. Once he had got me up there Kelly knew that I would never come down by the steps and after such a public announcement I was trapped.

The pool, set in the middle of lovely gardens, was only 25 metres long. It had been built hurriedly to allow the Egyptian team to train for the 1936 Olympics. Climbing the vertical ladder to the 10 metre platform took forever and I hung on tight to the metal rungs. Standing back on the board I could see no water, only the gardens. Behind me the Nile flowed swiftly by.

I walked cautiously to the end of the board and peered over: the pool looked so small that I was convinced I would miss the deep end altogether. Below the crowd was cheering after Kelly had announced that it was my first dive at this height. Heart in mouth I took off, lifted up and held, arms and legs stretched hard, toes pointed. It seemed an eternity and my legs were rising, rising, rising. They had to be stopped or I would land flat on my back. One arm flailed hopefully for control and I entered the water in the nick of time, over but not disastrously so. After that, of course, I was hooked on 10 metre diving but always treated it with the greatest caution and respect. Nothing concentrates the mind so much as the discipline of fright!

These open air swimming pools closed for the winter and on 3 November 1937 the athletic season started. It began with the first open women's athletic meeting organised by the Egyptian Athletic Federation at the Ma'adi Club ground. I won five open events as I did again the following January. On 27 February 1938 at the first athletic championships of Egypt held at the National Sporting Club I again won five open events, the 60, 100 and 300 metres and the high and long jump. Ma'adi won the relay. *La Bourse Egyptienne* wrote of a 'grand triumph'; the *Egyptian Mail* of a 'star performer'. The results found their way into the *News Chronicle* at home.

During that time I was learning two dances for the Cairo Amateur Dramatic Society's production of *The Vagabond King* which opened at the Opera House on 9 March. I was principal dancer in a ballet dance and in a gypsy number. I had been attending dancing school from an early age to learn ballet and tap dancing. At another gymkhana in March I won the Arab horse race on a beautiful thoroughbred that did all the work while I just stuck on. Although I could ride well I knew nothing about racing.

The season started again with a gala at Ma'adi pool when my first real swimming training began too. Kelly asked me to swim a length of the pool, 33⅓ metres, slowly. At the end he asked for another, then another and another which is how I began to swim between twenty and forty lengths of the bath training for the 100 metre crawl. If he had asked me to swim thirty lengths straight off, I would have been appalled by the boredom of it. It was not until much later in life that I learned the need for keeping going.

In June 1938 we went home to England for three months. Everyone there seemed to have heard of me through the press. I joined the Isander Ladies Diving Club and the Mermaid Swimming Club, both of which were very good to me, and I turned up at Wembley pool for training all day. At fourteen I was much younger than the English swimmers and divers who were pretty formidable too. Clearly I had a lot more training ahead but I still managed to come fifth in the 3 metre springboard National Diving Championships at Wembley that year. Then I entered for the 100 yards freestyle National Championships at Great Yarmouth. This was a sea water pool 100 yards long. I qualified but was unplaced in the finals.

Late that August we returned to Egypt a few days before the Egyptian championships at Alexandria. On 4 September I won the open 100 metres freestyle beating the Hungarian champion, Mrs Magda Lenky-Vafiades, who had set a world sprint record some years before. I also broke her record. In the same month I won the Egyptian diving championships for 3 metre springboard and 5 metre platform in Cairo. *La Bourse Egyptienne* reported 'fantastic Denise'. A cutting sent from America's *Parade of Youth* magazine read: 'Girl wins four titles just as a hobby, Egypt's best athlete at 14'. The following month I broke the 100 metre freestyle record at the Tewfikieh Club gala, again beating Magda Lenky-Vafiades. The *Egyptian Mail* headlined their report 'Denise Newman's Dazzling Dash'. A long article appeared in the *Echo Scolaire* magazine on 'our baby champion, swimming, diving, running, jumping, dancing and riding'; and *Actualities* newspaper, asked 'what will our young prodigy do for us next?'.

On 19 October an article in the *Daily Herald* by the well-known English swimming coach W. J. (Bill) Howcroft, who later became my trainer, was headed, 'Swimming Find of All Time'. He went on:

> Denise Newman's latest performance in swimming a 100 metre race in the sparkling time of 69¹⁄₁₀ seconds at Alexandria confirms the opinion expressed in these notes last month when the 14 year old English girl won the Egyptian 100 metre freestyle championship in 71⁶⁄₁₀ seconds. I wrote then that Miss Newman was the fleetest English girl of her age and perhaps the fastest in the world. I have seen all the post war champions in their early stages of development and have no hesitation in writing that the young newcomer has better credentials age for age than any European or World champion of the past twenty years. Miss Newman is a brighter prospect than Marie Braun, Yvonne Godard, Willy Den Ouden, Rie Mastenbroek and the reigning European champion Ragnhild Hveger when they broke into the racing game. A 14 year old schoolgirl who can sprint 100 metres in 69¹⁄₁₀ seconds after less than six months serious training is indeed the discovery of all time.

My diving training continued until I left Egypt. One day after a long session Kelly suddenly asked me to do a 2½ forward somersault tucked. At that time this was considered too dangerous for women and forbidden in competitions, but he said it was to improve my 1½ forward somersault. I was tired and for the first and only time refused. Angrily he said he would never ask me again, which upset me dreadfully. Next morning I dragged my long suffering mother to the deserted pool at 7.30, plucked up courage, shut my eyes tight while counting the spins and did it, with a straight entry as well. When I went on to show Kelly later in the day, I was so excited and he so pleased that I opened too soon and landed flat on my face. It was the only time I shut my eyes when diving – a mistake!

On 4 November another article appeared in the *Illustrated Sporting and Dramatic News* which read:

Denise Newman, a 14 year old English girl living with her parents in Ma'adi, Egypt, is heading for the highest honours in international swimming. In September she caused considerable surprise by winning the Egyptian 100 metre championship in 71⁶⁄10 seconds, an outstanding performance for a schoolgirl. The swim was enhanced by the fact that the Hungarian champion, Mrs Magda Lenky-Vafiades, who set up a world sprint record a few years ago, was placed second. Last month Denise Newman won a 100 metre scratch race at the Tewfikieh Swimming Gala in 69¹⁄10 seconds, the fastest swim ever recorded by a 14 year old in any part of the World . . . outstanding Olympic prospect, eligible to swim for Great Britain in the 1940 Olympic Games by her birth qualifications but it is obvious that the Egyptian Swimming Association will press their claim for her to swim for the country where she lives.

In November 1938, however, we returned to England for good. 'Denise Newman will be lost to Egypt' was the press comment, while Reuters reported 'British girl athlete prodigy coming home . . . Miss Denise Newman's feats in Egypt . . . distinguished herself in swimming, diving, riding and athletics etc'. That was the end of my formal schooling, at the age of fourteen. I was in the right class for my age group in spite of all my other activities and despite often missing homework to go riding. It was a pity I did not stay on to finish my education, which would have stood me in good stead later.

England

I hated England. We landed in a winter that was cold, dark and claustrophobic, with too much travelling just to train, unlike Ma'adi where I had only to hop on my bike to get to the pool. As Wembley pool was a skating rink in winter, my training was in smelly old London baths such as the one in Buckingham Palace Road. Mr Howcroft, by then quite elderly, became my swimming coach. Thirty lengths in that overheated pool were drearily uninspiring.

Diving training was in the Marshall Street baths behind Libertys. John (Spider) Webb, my new diving coach, was available only after his day's work as a physiotherapist and at weekends. He, like all coaches, generously, patiently gave time free to international potentials. Spider was an excellent coach. The depth at the baths was nine feet, the minimum for the 3 metre (10 feet) springboard and 5 metre platform. Learning new dives when I might be out of control on entry meant I had to avoid hitting my head on the bottom.

Marshall Street was an exceptionally draughty pool where we hung about shivering awaiting our turn on the boards. Muscles soon stiffened to a point where it became difficult and even dangerous to dive. Suddenly the divers vanished and I found them lobster pink squashed in a shallow square hot pot adjoining the spectator seats. The water was scorching, and after boiling ourselves we started diving again until we refroze, then back to the hot pot.

Although galas were often held at Marshall Street baths it was not a fast pool. There was no gutter trough at the sides so we were forced to swim back in our own wash. I won a good many Mermaid Club events in 1939 for both junior and senior swimming and diving and broke the senior 100 yard record. At the same time I studied ballet, tap and character dancing at the Judith Espinosa School of Dancing off Oxford Street and was taught ballet by the marvellous Judith herself; but ballet meant breaking the habits of my former tuition and starting again, which was hard going. Ballet is an excellent discipline for all sport bar swimming. My swimming coach wanted me to give up diving, riding and ballet as they stiffened my legs. My diving coach wanted me to give up swimming and concentrate on diving which I certainly preferred as it was more exciting. I quite liked competitive swimming but I disliked the endless slow lengths in training.

In spring of 1939 my father went out to the Anglo Iranian Oil Company's refinery in Abadan in Persia, as it was then called. My mother rented a house in Wembley to be near the pool where I could train that summer for the next Olympics to be held in Helsinki in 1940. There were no suitable country pools, where I would have been far happier. My times suggested that I would be chosen to swim for England before joining my father in Abadan. Long days were spent training in both swimming and diving. Meanwhile I was still dancing and riding when I had the chance. Perhaps I should have concentrated on one or the other; perhaps I was not properly advised: who knows? In England I felt less fit and lacked spontaneity.

In June 1939 I was selected to swim in the London v Paris match and in the relay at Marshall Street baths. I won the 100 yards freestyle and London won the relay. Next month I came second in the 100 yards freestyle at the National Championships at Minehead, one second behind the winner's time of 62⅘ seconds. I was still a junior competing in these open events.

I was chosen to swim freestyle in the England v Germany relay at Erfurt, Martin Luther's university town, 5–6 August 1939. This meant international status for me at fifteen and a white track suit top with Union flag and black track suit trousers, together with a navy blue blazer with a badge of a lion rampant with 1939, all embroidered in gold. Mr Howcroft wrote that I was lucky to make the grade in time as I had taken a good six months to acclimatise and found form only when I went to Minehead for the Nationals.

About twenty-four hours before we were due to leave for Germany by train, I had violent stomach pains. The doctor, realising I had set my heart on going, persuaded my mother it was an attack of colic. That sounded like horses so was bound to make sense! It was in fact a grumbling appendix. He gave me some medicine and said I was to avoid fruit and red meat, so off I went for the first time without my parents. I lived on fresh air and excitement as the food was dreadful. This was just before war broke out. The team went to some hall in Erfurt supposedly for a welcoming reception, but the speeches were shouted at us with much stomping and saluting. Luckily I knew no German. The competitors at the pool paraded in their national track suits. Our white tops stood out in the press photographs as we came to attention for the National Anthem. The Germans were noticeable by their outstretched arms, all 'Heil Hitlering'. The pool appeared to be a converted pond, and its muddy bottom made the water murky. It was inhibiting diving and swimming when you could see neither the bottom nor the turn coming up at the end of the pool.

The England v Denmark match was held 19–21 August; I was chosen to swim the freestyle (crawl) in the 4 × 100 metre relay. Then I won the Southern Counties junior 100 yards freestyle at Hastings pool. Although my appendix had calmed down, the time had come to have it out. I kept it in a bottle and was put out at not being able to go into full training for a few weeks. Apparently it was to let the muscles settle.

On 3 September 1939 war with Germany was declared.

Now there would be no Olympics, so in March 1940, when I was sixteen, my mother and I went out to Abadan to join my father. My brother stayed at home and joined the army.

4

Abadan, War and Olympics

Life in Abadan

In March 1940 preparations for joining my father in Abadan included the censorship of all papers and gramophone records. The ferry evaded two floating mines as we crossed from Harwich to the Hook of Holland where we caught a train first to Paris, then to Venice to await a ship. It was the lull before the storm of war that was shortly to engulf the continent of Europe. We called at Alexandria and Haifa and disembarked at Beirut from where we travelled on to Damascus by car. We then had another 450 miles to Baghdad by Nairn coach transport over the desert roads.

Pop met us at Baghdad and we stayed the night at the Zia Hotel where the barman was called Jesus. We caught a train to Basra and were then ferried across the Shatt al Arab river to Khorramshahr. A short journey by car along the dusty flat road brought us to Abadan. It compared unfavourably with Ma'adi, having no character whatsoever. Our bungalow at Braim, upwind of the oil refinery, I am glad to say, was near the swimming pool. A mixture of Arabs and Persians lived in the bazaar, but I found the latter rather dour and humourless.

I would have liked to explore the countryside, particularly as I love Persian carpets, but only went as far as Anglo Iranian's Ahwaz and Masjid i Suleiman oil fields. We flew in the small company aeroplane between the hills and mountains as the plane could not climb over them. Our Iraqi servants were highly amused by our Arabic until they saw Egyptian films in the bazaar and said incredulously, 'they speak the same Arabic as you'.

The pool was fine for swimming but of inadequate depth and lacking proper diving boards. The 1 metre springboard was passable but the only other board was useless. I kept up basic training on the 1 metre but it was really the end of my diving, and there was no competition in swimming.

I managed to get some riding, but the desert between Abadan and Khorramshahr and alongside the tributaries of the Shatt al Arab was flat, barren and bleak with a few sparse date palms and nowhere much to go. There were club dances and the open air cinema where you sat swathed in mosquito netting and covered in citronella cream against the mosquitoes, malarial or otherwise, which bred in the nullas (ditches). I was rarely bitten, but my father caught malaria badly and was sent to convalesce in India for four weeks. In February 1941 we flew by Imperial Airways flying boat from Basra to Karachi where we disembarked for a few hours. I looked for the nearest place to swim, which was in a fast flowing river. The water was pitch black so I abandoned diving off the 5 metre board in favour of swimming against the strong current. Sprinting flat out to gain ground slowly against the stream was a salutary experience.

We caught a small Tata Airways plane to Bombay but engine trouble brought us down in the Sind desert. Here we waited in the walled city of Bhuj belonging to the Maharajah of Kutch while another and smaller plane apparently tied up with bits of string came to our rescue. We landed safely in

Bombay despite a tyre bursting as we touched down. We spent some time there and then went to Poona for two weeks before returning to Iran.

In August 1941 the allies occupied Persia to keep the country from falling into German hands. Unbeknown to us, British forces invaded Abadan from the Gulf to seize the refinery from the resisting Iranians. We awoke with the noise of shooting in the lane outside. Our telephone lines had been cut and the servants could not get through with our daily provisions, so we had very little to eat. Bullets were whistling through the garden, but during the lulls my parents and I made dashes to and from the detached cookhouse to cook such food as we had. Iranian soldiers had barricaded themselves in a block of flats nearby and it took most of the day to get them to surrender. There were also several Iranian soldiers dead in the road outside the garden. We went to tend them but it was too late. The fighting ended that evening and order was restored.

The Rajputana Rifles, the Gurkhas, the Sikhs and the Kumaan Rifles were stationed in Abadan in turn. At the age of seventeen I met my future husband who was in the Rajputana Rifles.

The Abadan Dramatic Society put together an all woman revue to tour Iraq giving shows for the forces stationed there. They called it Nomensa, after ENSA (Entertainment National Service Association), which gave variety shows for the troops both at home and abroad during the war. Our troupe had no men! I was recruited for my dancing. We travelled Iraq and received a rapturous welcome everywhere. No doubt the cheerful, colourful all girl musical show obscured any shortage of theatrical talent.

However, I grew restless during my two and a half years in Abadan. I wanted to train for a useful wartime job. When the French mistress became ill I was asked to teach ten- and eleven-year olds at the local English school. The kids wanted to talk only about swimming and diving but I diverted that to after lesson time. The school's managing committee reported a great improvement in the children's French, which cheered me up. I was also asked to coach the Iranian students at Abadan University for diving. They were enthusiastic although there was only a 1 metre springboard. One of the Abadan University Iranian tutors gave me instruction in written and spoken Persian which share a vocabulary, unlike the Arabic in Egypt where the spoken language is different from the written. I found it interesting but hard work.

Back to England

My father had a recurrence of malaria followed by pneumonia and pleurisy. This meant he could not stay on in the intense heat of the Persian Gulf, but had to be invalided back to England. We left Abadan in November 1942 but it took us six months to get home because we were classed as non-essential civilians in wartime. We eventually sailed from the Gulf in a small vessel that had accommodation for six first class passengers, the rest being literally deck passengers. There were no blackout arrangements so when the sun went down we lived in the dark with difficulty. The jovial white-haired captain was long overdue for retirement. Escorted part of the way by an Indian naval vessel, we took three weeks to reach Bombay, where again I was asked to give diving exhibitions.

At last we found a ship bound for Cape Town and went from the ridiculous to the sublime. The *Cape Town Castle* was a great peacetime luxury liner and apart from the blackout nothing much had changed. The swimming pool was in the bowels of the ship. I gravitated there, though it was not the best of places to be if the ship were torpedoed. It took a fortnight to reach Cape Town where we stayed before moving to Stellenbosch which had a suitable swimming pool. It was a mistake. Although an enchanting sleepy village surrounded by mountains, Stellenbosch had a large Afrikaner population, many of whom were anti-British and pro-Nazi. I saw them saluting German prisoners of war walking in the streets. Stellenbosch University pool, open to the public, was run to racist and sexist rules: 'Slegs Vir Blankies' (whites only), and women only sessions which excluded even two-year-old boys.

Longstreet baths in Cape Town asked me to give a swimming and diving exhibition on 9 January 1943. This invitation was made much of in the *Cape Town Times*, which reported on the 'brilliant young swimmer' and 'wonder girl from Egypt who carried everything before her in Egyptian swimming and diving championships, coached by Kelly and at 14 years, 100 metres freestyle in 69.1 seconds and described as the fastest girl in the world for her age. Represented England against Germany, France and Denmark'. After so much publicity I was concerned, as I had already explained that less than seven feet of water was too shallow for diving from the 3 metre springboard and that I had intended only to swim. Under pressure on the day I performed what dives I could in safety, feet first, which appeared to satisfy the spectators.

Johannesburg invited me to give a diving exhibition and compete in an invitation 100 yards race at Ellis Park bath in aid of war funds. Although I was nineteen years old my mother was invited as chaperone, and we set off for a 900 mile train journey across the lovely Great Karoo arriving in Johannesburg thirty-six hours later where I received a wonderful welcome. Ellis Park bath was modern. The diving pool with 3 metre and 10 metre boards was separate from the swimming pool, which relieved you of the worry of hitting someone diving under the board just as you were taking off.

Standing back for a run off the 10 metre platform, you cannot see the water below and are dependent on the attendant or your coach keeping a sharp look out. I won the 100 yards freestyle and broke the bath record in a poor time, as I was now feeling the effects of the 6000 feet altitude. Next stop was Pretoria where I won the 100 yards invitation race in a slightly improved time.

Back in Stellenbosch I was asked to give an exhibition of swimming and diving at their University pool. When the posters advertising the event went up, I was shown as champion of Egypt, my English connections omitted. Incensed, I bought an extra-large Union flag and sewed it on my international white track suit top. Now there could be no doubt I was British. Two Dutch instructors attached to the University, a man and a woman, practised with me and enthusiastically joined in the diving exhibition to keep continuity going for the audience. It went off well and we enjoyed it, but there were strong protests afterwards from students' parents that a man had been in the pool with two women – disgraceful!

I was asked to return to Johannesburg for another gala on 10 March in aid of the Royal Air Force. A few days before I was due to leave Stellenbosch I hurt my back fooling around with friends. Next day I was staggering about like an old woman. How could I hope to dive? My mother was persuaded to take me to an osteopath who, although blind, promptly diagnosed the trouble and snicked my back into position. I walked away as if nothing had happened.

We had news of a ship to take us home, so we moved back to Cape Town where I volunteered to help with meals for the troops. I was up at 4 a.m. to scrub and peel potatoes and then serve breakfast. What I lacked in finesse I made up for in speed. As I could not bear to keep people waiting, I loaded a large tray with plates of eggs and bacon only to find I was unable to hold it in one hand while I moved the plates on to

32

the table. There was not an inch of space anywhere so I balanced the tray on a serviceman's head. He did not seem to mind.

The *Dempo*, Rotterdam-Lloyd line, was a medium sized ship carrying cargo, mail and passengers, many of whom were on active service. There was also a great number of women and children. At that time losses from enemy submarines were devastating both in the North Atlantic and off the coast of West Africa. The usual port of call at Freetown in Sierre Leone was abandoned, and we sailed non-stop for England without convoy on a long roundabout route.

The *Dempo* berthed safely at Liverpool in May 1943 and we caught an overnight sleeper to London where I set about joining up. The Army was full up and the Navy offered only truck driving, so I went to the Air Ministry who were interested in my Arabic and Persian and promptly tested me on both. Since it was sprung on me there was no time to get nervous. As I was leaving they asked if I would like to learn Japanese. Thinking they were pulling my leg, I gave an airy but affirmative answer and ended up in the Foreign Office as a nineteen-year-old civilian.

While waiting for security clearance I won the Middlesex County Championships for 100 yards freestyle and springboard diving. Directly my clearance came through I reported to Bletchley Park and stayed there a couple of weeks before going to Bedford to start a crash course in written Japanese. Normally such studies took two and a half years but were concentrated here into six months. The other students were graduates. Exams took place every three weeks and if you did not keep up you were asked to leave. I was in at the deep end again, my formal education having more or less stopped at fourteen. If I found Japanese grammar complicated and the amount of vocabulary to absorb each night formidable, I did enjoy drawing the beautiful Japanese characters using a

33

brush with each stroke in its proper order. We learned about one thousand characters, although you need to know some five thousand to read the newspapers without constant use of a dictionary.

I then started work at Bletchley Park itself where I was involved in the Japanese cipher section. This work was secret until the early 1970s when Bletchley's role became public knowledge. The work was fascinating, but the long hours with little time off and food rationing made it fairly exhausting, and at the age of twenty-one I caught measles of all things. We had missed the terrible bombing by the Luftwaffe and had arrived back in England in time for the doodle bugs (flying bombs) and the rockets, but I was only affected by them when I went up to London to see my parents. Our family was lucky enough to survive the war.

As Japan capitulated, I married Vyvyan St Aubyn Hubbard at St George's, Hanover Square, in August 1945. We really knew little about each other, which perhaps partly explains why it all turned out so unhappily. Demobbed as a major just before my daughter Geraldine was born on 8 June 1946, he first tried his hand at banking before starting at Emmanuel College, Cambridge, in October 1947, to read architecture.

Most undergraduates then were older than usual because of the war, married with children and living out of college. Accommodation was short, often squalid, lacking facilities and expensive. We were extremely hard up, and I was thoroughly undomesticated. However, I was determined my family should not suffer and I learned fast to cook, clean, knit and look after a baby properly. I did not like domestic work much and still do not.

The Olympics

There was no suitable pool in Cambridge but my club gave me the opportunity to train in London two days a week in preparation for the 1948 Olympics. Could I make a comeback? I had not trained since 1939 apart from three months in South Africa, when I had no coach to teach me new dives and keep me up to scratch. Twice a week I took Geraldine to London by train where my parents looked after her while I practised, mostly at Marshall Street or at Ironmonger Row baths and occasionally at Isleworth. Wembley was now a skating rink all the year round which meant there was no 10 metre board near enough to practise apart from the muddy, murky Highgate ponds which I funked using.

At the Amateur Swimming Association (ASA) national championships at Hastings in July 1947 Geraldine stole the show by swimming before she could walk properly. At thirteen months she was so energetic and excited she just about swam on her own. In the springboard diving I came third but was unplaced in the highboard.

The divers went to the open-air pond at Dawdon Colliery near Durham for training and stayed with miners' families for several days. There we had the opportunity of going down the mine, one mile down and two miles out under the sea. They were blasting at the coal face, and I was allowed to drive and manoeuvre the rocker shovel which picked up the result of the blast and threw it back over your head. I have never forgotten the cheerful friendliness of those colliers battling away unseen and unsung in their terrible black caverns: such a hard life.

Next came Blackpool in April 1948 for intensive training and pre-Olympic trials. There were new dives to learn and perfect in the few days of the Easter holiday before the assessment competition. It was always scary learning a new dive off the 10 metre board. You could afford no mistakes from that height. The timing had to be correct and the change of timing from 3 metre springboard to 10 metre highboard was considerable. The lower board had the spring to set the hips spinning for somersaults, but it was harder to get the turns under way from the solid highboard base. Spider, my coach, would not tolerate any dithering on the top board. While I tried to pluck up courage he started to walk out, and I was off and into the dive at full speed. To my amazement I won the highboard trials and came second in the springboard. My optional dives for the highboard included the beautiful reverse dive straight. I stood on the end of the 10 metre board facing forward, lifted up into a plain jump, arms in the swallow position, hips rising fast with head forward, looking at my feet. I held that position until I felt myself balanced at the top of my height on a pivot before descent started; dropped my head backwards into a back dive towards the board, looked for the water and closed for entry. At the National Championships I came third in both events and as a result was chosen to represent Great Britain for the Olympics in the 10 metre highboard event – great excitement.

The Games took place in London from 29 July to 14 August 1948. The opening ceremony march past was most impressive, with each country's team led by a standard bearer. We marched to the music of the massed bands of the Brigade of Guards with a fanfare of trumpets sounded by the Trumpeter of the Household Cavalry as the Olympic flags were raised in the arena. In ancient Greece the arrival of doves was a signal that the Games had begun and that peace in the land must prevail. Britain released seven thousand pigeons. The torch bearer entered the stadium. Greece led the procession as originator of the Games. Great Britain, as host nation, brought up the rear, and heads turned to the right on passing the royal stadium to salute King George VI. There were more than four thousand competitors from fifty-eight countries excluding Germany and Japan, who were not invited, and the USSR, which was not then part of the Olympic movement.

We were billeted from 27 July in the Domestic Science School in Eccleston Square, London. I was on the fifth floor with no lift, which was not good for diving training. Several of us shared a bleak room, and the bright naked light bulb was left on until the early hours as some girls seemed to manage late nights as well. I tried to get to sleep early as the divers had to be up at 5 a.m. to practise before the swimmers started. There was no separate diving pool. Rushing to the baths before breakfast and before our bodies were physically awake and throwing ourselves off the 10 metre board was not a good idea. It caused us strain and injury. The authorities would not allow our own coaches to continue training us in spite of our protests. An excellent former highboard diver was appointed overall coach, but we needed individual coaching at that critical time. As a result I was overtrained and my muscles had begun to complain at the stress and the early hours.

Our swimming costumes were the biggest joke. Made according to international rules, about two inches down the leg and cut fairly high at the back, clearly they had not been modified since the Ark. The dull navy-blue clinging material had been especially woven and made us look like twelve-year-old schoolgirls in vests and knickers. It did absolutely nothing to enhance the figure. To top it, a huge Union flag was plastered across our bosoms like a breast plate. The North Americans and the Mexicans had attractively cut modern swim suits made of satin. I swopped a rather nice silver bracelet and brooch for a couple. Unfortunately they were pale blue and yellow respectively, so could not be used for competitions.

One of the nicest things about these international events

was meeting old friends and competitors from all over the world. Kelly, my Egyptian coach, came as a trainer; it was a great pleasure to see him again and also the Egyptian team.

The first part of the 10 metre highboard event took place on 6 August. Spider had insisted on my taking the previous day off for rest to prevent me from getting stale. The result was I was on form and was lying fifth at the end of the first three dives, 2½ points behind the American leader. However, as I entered the water during that third dive I felt a searing pain in my shoulder. The pain was so intense I had great difficulty using the arm in the last compulsory dive and went over on entry. My shoulder muscle was torn. I was strapped up for my last two optional dives, a reverse dive straight and a flying 1½ forward somersault piked but was barely able to raise my arm, lost control and dropped to eleventh place in the finals. The other two British girls came tenth and twelfth.

Despite the setback I was one of two high divers chosen for the England v Denmark match in Copenhagen, 1–3 October. The Danish girl who was third in the Olympics highboard won the 10 metre diving, I came second. My shoulder no longer affected my diving at all but ached dreadfully at night when it stiffened.

Back in Cambridge, the Victoria Cinema screened the full-length Olympic film in which I was to be seen diving off the 10 metre board. The manager invited me to appear on stage where he interviewed me and presented complimentary tickets to all my friends. It had been a busy year.

5

Family Life

We found a half acre or so of land going cheap on the outskirts
of Little Shelford village, five miles south of Cambridge. My
husband bought three army huts for about £30 and designed
a one-storey house with a large sitting room, dining room
and three bedrooms. There were enough good bits from the
prefabricated buildings for the outside which was overlaid
with mesh, cement rendered and whitewashed by the build-
ers. Inside walls were plastered breeze block. As many floors
as we were allowed were made of wood, still rationed, and
the rest were concrete. The joke was that in one of the huts
there was a pin-up of me sitting on the end of a diving board
in my bathing costume, which had been on the front cover
of *Illustrated Weekly*. Clearly the huts had been meant for us.
Twin brothers, twenty-one years old and impossible to tell
apart, built the house in the morning, acted as undertakers
in the afternoon and spent their evenings playing in a dance
band. To save rent we moved in once the roof was on and
camped out while the house was built around us. It was not
much fun and bitterly cold. Geraldine went to my parents
until the floors were in, the water connected and the place
vaguely habitable.

I became pregnant with Hugh. Geraldine, who was only three, became desperately ill. For some time I had noticed that she appeared to have something up her nose and had asked the doctor to look. He dismissed the idea and did nothing. Even though her temperature rose to 105°F still the doctor would not call in a second opinion or agree to her going to hospital; so we took her there without his permission. They were horrified: at first they thought it was poliomyelitis, then meningitis; finally they diagnosed osteomyelitis, inflammation of the marrow of her hip bone. Not only did penicillin save her life but it avoided the need for a hip operation, which might have left her with a permanent limp. The hospital rule, experimental at that time, was that parents were not allowed to visit. That upset me a good deal and turned out to be a mistake. She must have felt abandoned.

When after a few weeks she came out of hospital she was skin and bone. She had seldom cried before and was normally a happy child, talkative and singing, but now she screamed interminably. She refused to walk, although apparently there was no physical reason why she should not. The hospital staff had been good to her but she had been held down screaming for the necessary but painful penicillin injections and probably spoilt with sweets to compensate. I despaired.

Geraldine's room was painted in time for her return and we bought her a new doll. One day, I sat her on her little chair with a bucket of water for the doll's bath just out of reach, went into the garden and looked in through the glass doors. She was so absorbed with the doll that she walked over to the bucket quite unconsciously. I was relieved and set about feeding her up, but still she was not fully recovered as her snoring could be heard through closed doors. Once again the doctor said, 'wait and see', so we took her straight back to hospital and again I insisted there was something up her nose. They X-rayed her but nothing showed. After probing they brought down wads of cotton wool and paper that she had been stuffing up her nose over a period of time, which must have become infected. After that, all was well and when next she went for a check up they wrote 'a different child' in her notes.

Hugh was born on 13 March 1950, grew fast and was walking by nine months but considered it unnecessary to talk. His sister, although much lighter, had not been interested in walking that young but talked at nine months and is still a chatterbox. Hugh grew up to think a five mile run was a short distance.

When I was seven months pregnant with Hugh the Mermaid Swimming Club had asked me if I would swim in the Club medley relay race at the Nationals at Morecambe, Lancashire and also enter for the National Diving Championships on 24 July. I entered them in a state of euphoria but with little practice four months after Hugh's birth and surprised myself by winning the 3 metre springboard. Selected for the England v Germany match at Oberhausen, near Dusseldorf, in September, I came third in the springboard. Tessie Bartley, honorary secretary and treasurer for the Mermaid Club for many, many years, wrote on behalf of the committee to congratulate me on winning the National 3 metre springboard and on coming third in the match against Germany. 'I think you must have established a record by being one of the last English swimmers to compete in Germany in August 1939 and one of the first to go after the war', she wrote. 'I don't think anyone else has done the two'. I was asked to be guest of honour at the club dinner that year, and in February 1951 the committee presented me with the Club Coronation Cup awarded at its discretion for 'an outstanding achievement during the 1950 season'.

There was talk of the 1952 Olympic Games in Helsinki but I had no opportunity to train and came third in the trials. In order to economise, the Olympic Committee decided to send the first two competitors from each event instead of the usual three. As in 1940 I missed Helsinki.

In 1950 my husband had got his degree and then went up to London twice a week to the Royal Academy on a Lawrence grant for the next two years to continue his architectural studies. When his time at the Royal Academy was up he had yet to pass his final exams after the five years it then took to become an architect. In the meantime he found a job with an architectural practice in Portsmouth. We sold our house Windrift at a profit and moved to really grotty lodgings in Southsea while we looked for a place to buy before our profit was exhausted. The job paid so little. In September 1953 my husband found work in Chichester where we rented a tiny furnished semi-detached old house opposite the Cathedral, with an outside loo and no bathroom. To our horror the clock on the Cross boomed out midnight as we fell into bed exhausted from the move. Amazingly, though, we never again noticed it. After a spartan six months we moved to an unfurnished first floor flat going cheaply on the other side of the road. Geraldine started school at Lavant House, catching the bus outside the flat each morning. I toured the sale rooms to bid for job lots taking Hugh and Claude, our rescued greyhound-cum-lurcher. Claude always insisted on lying full length across the gangways where everyone admired him and good naturedly stepped over him. At one country house sale I fell asleep in the arm chair which came up for auction, 'but not the sleeping beauty in it!' I managed to get enough together to live with even if we did not like much of it.

We looked for land on which to build and found it in Bosham about fifty yards from the water. Land was cheap in those days before Bosham became fashionable. Over a third of an acre cost us £400 and the house was built without frills for £2,200. We determined to clear the builder's rubble

42

ourselves but it stayed there for a long time. The house had a large sitting room, dining room, three double bedrooms and a single. I made all the curtains, linings and bed covers. As the windows were quite large the mileage on my ancient sewing machine, 'donkety donk', seemed endless. We moved in on 1 July 1955.

A full mortgage was obtained as the house was valued at more than it cost us, and no deposit was needed; the arrangement was that only the interest on the loan would be paid but no capital repayments made. Even so we were hard pressed to pay that interest. After qualifying as an architect in 1954 my husband changed jobs pretty frequently. By now he was going up to London daily before deciding to start his own practice in Chichester.

Bosham, a beautiful village at the top of Chichester harbour, where people just popped in, was the friendliest place I had known in England. The children and their friends congregated at home just as I and my friends had in my childhood in Ma'adi and romped with Claude the lurcher and the cats. Poohdy, the tortoiseshell pooh-cat, ruled my life and always got her way. By now Hugh (Boo), aged five, had joined Geraldine (Jo) at Lavant House and the era of the rabbits began. Jo brought home a lovely coffee-coloured buck rabbit, Thumper, just before the holidays, saying there was no one to look after the rabbits once the boarders had left. I hate to have animals in cages so he romped round the house during the day playing with Claude's tail. The poor dog was highly embarrassed as he had been taught to chase rabbits. Thumper was taken out in a harness and lead, and if you knew how many dogs there were in Bosham you would have been amazed at Jo's nerve.

Bosham was a lovely place in which to bring up children, with the tidal waters of the creek, its ever changing colours and moods, and the Downs to the north. There were no street lights, little traffic and few houses then. It was full of flowers and trees and so like Ma'adi with only the desert missing. I was even lucky enough to get some riding occasionally, thanks to generous girl friends.

Hugh started at Oakwood prep school as a day boy at seven years old before he became a boarder at eleven. For his last two years of day school he insisted on running there and back, about three miles each way, which started him off on cross-country running. He was only about eight or nine but he was determined to do it – all very worrying. Meanwhile Jo passed her eleven-plus exam and went on to Chichester High School.

I was asked occasionally to give diving exhibitions at Hilsea pool, Cosham near Portsmouth, the only ten metre board within fifteen miles. In July 1961 I opened the 25 metre open air swimming pool at the Chichester High School for Girls. I was able to advise on where to get a good regulation one metre springboard, the maximum height for the limited depth of water available with their slender funds. I was asked to give an exhibition of twelve dives, and Geraldine was detailed to stand by with towels. 'You shiver just like your daughter,' commented the games mistress. In October 1963 I gave a display of diving at the opening of the new Portsmouth swimming pool, but sailing now was taking over. On instead of in it, water was still the fatal attraction.

6

To Sea in *Pintail*

English Channel voyaging

In 1956 we met Andrew Reid and his beloved *Pintail*, sail number Z20, a Chichester Harbour Z class wooden clinker built sloop, overall length 15 feet (4.57 metres), beam six feet. A racing boat of her time, she was built by Harry Feltham of Portsmouth in 1935. Andrew or John, as he was known in Bosham to distinguish him from his father, also called Andrew Reid, had made several voyages in *Pintail* to Weymouth and the Channel Islands, even though she was only a day boat. He had repositioned the tall spruce mast further forward to correct her weather helm. The cockpit seats were slatted and she was only half decked so there was little shelter except for a small canvas spray hood which covered the forward part of the open cockpit.

In the summer of 1957 we sailed her in Chichester harbour, a beautiful area of sheltered water. We would either anchor or beach her and swim. The currents at East Head were strong and the beach shelved steeply, so I went in the water with the children to keep constant guard as well as to play.

During that winter Aeromarine Ltd. fitted an open-ended

coach roof (cab) to *Pintail*, and Freezers fixed aluminium rails round the cockpit. Royal blue canvas dodgers were lashed to these, providing some protection for those in the cockpit. To the open cab was secured a canvas cover on aluminium supports which could be pulled aft in rough weather.

In 1958 I made my first mini-voyage in *Pintail* outside the shelter of Chichester harbour from Bosham to Yarmouth, Isle of Wight. John was an engineer working in London. By the time he had arrived in Bosham and changed into sea gear and the three of us had rowed out to *Pintail*, stowed and prepared for sea, it was getting on for midnight. It was over four miles to the harbour entrance; the wind died so *Pintail* was anchored off Hayling Island where a very strong ebb tide was running. As I was not impressed with the cramped conditions inside the boat, I opted to sleep in the open, wrapped in as many warm clothes as I could find, not having funds for oilskins. I was dimly aware of John tramping over me through the night, letting out more and more anchor rope as the wind rose, and of agitated conversation as to whether the anchor would hold. It held and we set sail again at first light for Yarmouth. The wind had abated and it became a lovely day. I dived over the side for a swim between Chichester harbour entrance and the Forts.

Pintail sailed to Weymouth, Cherbourg and St Malo in France and to St Peter Port and Gorey in the Channel Islands. School and university friends of John's joined as crew, as did my husband, but I was left behind on the long voyages. I was rather fed up since I did not go on holidays; although we did now have some marvellous weekends sailing in the Solent in *Pintail*. John finally took pity on me and in 1959 invited me to go along. Geraldine and Hugh stayed with friends while four of us set off from Bosham towards Weymouth, a long haul for a 15 foot boat.

During the previous winter John had worked on *Pintail*.

The slatted seats had given way to well-made, varnished lockers. She slept four in harbour. There were two berths forward with sleeping bags on lilos on either side of the centreplate box. There were comfortable sea berths too under the little cuddy, once you had struggled to get your hips through the low opening under the foredeck. In harbour the locker seats aft with foam cushions served as the other two berths with a fitted canvas awning thrown over aluminium coat hangers suspended from the boom and tied down to form a cockpit tent. It was very cosy once the *gaz* lamp was lit. At sea on long passages, two crew were on watch and two off watch in the forward sea berths.

Pintail was equipped with as much gear as a well-found five ton yacht, cleverly stowed under the berth boards forward, which John had made, and in the cockpit lockers. She carried fathoms of anchor rope, self-inflatable life jackets and a self-inflatable liferaft, an outboard motor, fuel and one of the first Brookes and Gatehouse direction finding (DF) sets; also large red, green and white torches to show in sufficient time on the approach of a ship to avert collision, and a large quantity of Admiralty charts as well as almanacs and pilot books. The ex-RAF grid steering compass in a wooden box bolted to the cockpit sole gave even less room to move with four crew on board. Cooking was on a small camping *gaz* stove which you gripped with your heels as you sat in the cockpit. When it was too windy the flame blew out, and rough weather made the stove unstable. The trim or balance of the boat at sea was vital, and one practically had to ask permission to move for fear of capsizing.

This passage to Weymouth was my first experience of open sea work in a small vessel. It was rough rounding St Albans Head, not a place to be in strong weather with wind against tide conditions over an uneven seabed kicking up a steep, irregular sea through which *Pintail* crashed and bucked. I sat in the cockpit wearing a long oilskin coat given to me, but lacking oily trousers and boots, I was soon very wet. I decided it was like swimming and dozed off. When I woke I asked if Weymouth was round the corner. 'If we ever get round the corner', the crew groaned. I was blissfully ignorant of the sea's dangers. Being an open boat, *Pintail* had to be reefed down early, particularly in a seaway when the water was rough, for fear of being overwhelmed. It was a specialist job knowing how much sail she could carry safely in the varying conditions experienced, but John was a competent and experienced open boat seaman. To my delight the voyage resulted in my being asked again because I did not mind cooking and remained cheerful when the going got rough, windy and wet.

We left *Pintail* at Weymouth and returned the following weekend to take her on to the Channel Islands, setting out in the early hours of the morning. Dawn broke miserable and grey over a lumpy, dreary sea. Starting from as far west as Weymouth gave us a slant to the prevailing southwesterly winds, enabling us to sail the track of 80 miles or so outside the Casquets and through the Little Russell channel to St Peter Port, Guernsey. We arrived late that night cramped and exhausted, but pleased with our successful voyage. *Pintail* may have been the greyhound of her day when she was stripped for racing, but now, with cruising gear carefully stowed to ballast her and a crew of four, her maximum speed through the water under her original rig was 4½ knots. John was both an excellent skipper and a hard task master. The vessel's safety came first and we had to jump to it. Voyaging in little *Pintail* was not everyone's idea of a good time, but it was good training. Despite having a great sense of humour and fun, on passage John was always quiet and preoccupied with plans which anticipated the dangers and limited the risks. When her sails were reefed right down in strong winds *Pintail* would find it difficult to claw off a lee shore, so it was vital to have plenty of sea room by keeping well offshore.

The little Seagull outboard motor with ten gallons of fuel in cans was available when needed to give us a range of about 100 miles. Setting it up in any sort of seaway was dicey. John would balance himself on the after deck and rails to position the outboard in its bracket. How he did not overbalance and follow it down into the deep in hot pursuit I will never know. Nowadays it is permanently secured over the stern: simpler and safer.

Early next morning we left St Peter Port bound for Gorey, an enchanting small harbour in Jersey. It was a long, rough haul when the wind turned against the tide, but I was ignorant of the difficulties of this wild ride. John appeared to have forgotten about breakfast. Apart from an early morning coffee after a short night's sleep, we had not eaten since the previous evening. I was too polite to suggest it and grew hungrier and hungrier as the seas became rougher and rougher along Jersey's northern coast. Extricating the food from its forward stowage was complicated and required the skipper's permission as we had to move with great care to keep the boat balanced. Richard Tetley, an old friend of John's, and I had the capacity to sleep at any time in any position. Off watch and asleep upright in the cockpit we were suddenly hit hard on the back of our heads with what seemed to be a block of wood. It was a wave. John ordered lifejackets on, to my great excitement!

Short tacking we slowly worked our way eastwards hemmed in between the Paternoster rocks and the north shore of Jersey. Reefed right down and close hauled, we made excessive leeway in wind over tide conditions which made for a turbulent sea. Between St John's and Bonne Nuit Bay, the tidal stream turned against us, and though sailing furiously we could make no headway. However, the contrary tide now flowed in the same direction as the remorseless wind which smoothed the seas somewhat.

Off Gifford Bay John managed to get the outboard out of the locker and couple it on to the stern bracket and we motor sailed until we rounded the corner of Jersey off St Catherine's Bay, when we cut the motor and sailed again. Steering became difficult as we ran with the wind on the port quarter and a big following sea. *Pintail*'s rudder repeatedly came out of the water as the stern lifted to the overtaking waves. Despite downing the foresail altogether and reefing the mainsail to pocket handkerchief size, *Pintail* careered down wind only partly under control. In later years John added a drop rudder to give more depth and carried a drogue to stream astern to counter such conditions. It was too rough to gybe to enter Gorey harbour so we waited for a smooth patch between seas and tacked fast through the wind. We landed on the beach behind the breakwater exhausted, cold, wet, salty and hungry after the sixteen hour voyage. *Pintail* had no problems in this sheltered drying harbour as she had a lifting centreplate and could sit safely on the bottom.

The most tiring part at the end of any voyage in *Pintail* was extricating the coat hangers and tarpaulin to provide shelter for the night. By the time we had set it up, lashed it down and struggled out of our oilies, all in each other's way, we were even more exhausted. But the lantern had to be lit and a meal prepared, when all we really wanted was to collapse in a heap. That was impossible until we had retrieved the harbour equipment from under the forward berths. We left *Pintail* at Gorey. John and the others returned later and sailed her back to Bosham.

In 1960 we sailed to Cherbourg and berthed outside the yacht club near the town, long before the marina was built. As a working port Cherbourg was both attractive and interesting, busy with commercial and fishing vessels and passenger liners on the Atlantic run. At weekends the yacht club seemed packed with the British among whom were some familiar faces. After a few days we set sail for Deauville. It was so rough outside that we turned back, left *Pintail* and flew home. Later we returned and sailed her some 75 miles across the Baie de la Seine to lock in, twenty hours later, opposite the yacht club. Occasionally we had lunch at Les Trois Canards, a backstreet restaurant patronised by the working locals where we carried on animated discussions with everyone on all subjects in poor French. The expensive nightlife in the gambling port of Deauville–Trouville was beyond reach or desire.

After thirty-six hours tacking all the way back to Chichester harbour we sailed to Itchenor to clear Customs. In those days you were not allowed even to set foot on shore to telephone them. As there was no one within call we picked up a mooring, hoisted a yellow duster to serve as a quarantine flag, and hopefully blew our foghorn. Going ashore could have meant having the boat impounded. We were starving, exhausted and scruffy but lunch had to wait until Customs had been cleared. Two officers boarded us quickly and we offered to open the lockers and drag everything out from on and under the forward deckboards. However, they chose to check us out by engaging us in prolonged conversation. With five of us squashed in the cockpit, freeboard aft was short and balance precarious.

Later that summer John and my husband sailed *Pintail* (*Pinners*, as we called her) to Deauville again while the children and I flew from Lydd airport to join them. When they returned home to work, Hugh, Geraldine and I stayed on for a holiday living on board in the *bassin*, which was enormous fun. A furious gale blew up and Jo and I spent the night fending off in our pyjamas, our attempts to wake Hugh having failed. He sleeps with such gusto.

Early in 1961 John went off to work in Iran for a couple

of years and *Pintail* was laid up. We cruised occasionally on friends' yachts as we had no boat of our own. I started evening classes in basic navigation. In mid-1962 John returned from Iran on leave and sailed with friends to the Channel Islands and France, leaving *Pintail* at St Malo ready to take her through the canals to Vannes in the Gulf of Morbihan, some 132 miles.

In September we went out en famille to St Malo with the children looking forward to canal life. Hugh was the lock monkey scrambling up the sides to take our lines when no keeper was available and tying up each evening at six as traffic came to a halt. From St Malo we made our way first to Dinan where we entered the Ille et Rance canal to Rennes. That part had forty-seven locks including eleven in quick succession to reach the summit. Jo left us there to return to school and at sixteen years found it a great adventure making her own way back home. From Rennes to Redon there were twelve locks in the canalised part of the River Vilaine. We came out at the port of La Roche Bernard where we helped John re-step the mast which had been lowered at St Malo to enable us to pass under the canal bridges. Hugh and I returned home while John and my husband sailed to Vannes at the far end of the Gulf of Morbihan to lay *Pintail* up under cover for the winter.

His leave over, John went back to Iran. On returning to England in 1963 he went straight to Vannes to work on *Pintail*, sandpapering her, caulking the seams between planks, varnishing, painting, antifouling and re-rigging to get her ready for sea. Even today, fifty-five years old, she looks brand new.

In July, three of us set off to sail her back from France, a voyage of 465 nautical miles from Vannes to Bosham via Falmouth. We set off down the Gulf of Morbihan with its strong tidal streams, many islands and shallows and sailed out through the Passage de la Teignouse between Houat and

Quiberon. The wind died and the outboard failed intermittently passing through the Passage with its outlying rocks and tide rips and we had difficulty tacking into a 2 knot southwesterly wind. Eventually we reached the enchanting little port of Sauzon on the northeast side of Belle Isle where we anchored for the night.

Next day we set off towards the Raz de Sein on our passage home, but the strong northwesterly winds heading us and the rough seas drove us to take shelter at Port Tudy, Isle de Groix. It was too rough to reach the shore and the motion was relentless; thirty-six hours cooped up in a tiny vessel was taxing in the extreme. After a couple of days the wind abated and again we set off for the Raz de Sein under motor as it was dead calm and misty. Visibility deteriorated all day and by nightfall was down to 10 yards. We were too late for a fair tide through the Race so decided to put into Audierne. The approach buoy had a whistle, which we hoped to locate. All day we had maintained a meticulous plot of our estimated position and when it showed we must be nearing the buoy we switched off the outboard to listen: nothing. We started up, motored half a cable, switched off, listened. Taking soundings with the lead line we repeated this routine until the dying moan of a whistle could be heard broad on the port bow. Motoring on we picked up the elusive buoy and from there made for the safety of the outer anchorage which we reached by 0200 hours. We flaked out for a couple of hours without putting up the canvas cockpit cover. It was a cold, bleak and hungry sleep.

The Raz de Sein, five miles long and two miles wide, was ten miles from Audierne. The tidal stream rate is 6½ knots at springs when the overfalls can be dangerous. We set off against the tide so as to arrive at the Raz at slack water with the stream just turning north in our favour. Once through the channel we set sail for the fast flowing Chenal du Four between the French mainland and Ile d'Ouessant (Ushant). It was still calm and misty so we put into Camaret for provisions and fuel in case we needed to motor.

We set out at dusk and again visibility closed down. Motoring through the Chenal, the outboard blew the exhaust pipe off the cylinder block, and the ensuing cacophony compelled us to stop the engine in a strong cross tide which was rapidly carrying us out of the safe channel. John hung over the stern to effect repairs while the crew held on to his legs, and the motor was restarted just in time. Once through we were on our way across the Channel to Falmouth. It took us a day and a half to cover the 120 miles. Crossing the main shipping lanes in fog was alarming, as we would have had little time to alter course if a ship had loomed up out of the murk. Despite the dense fog a spanking easterly breeze persisted until we emerged into local patches of slightly better visibility when the wind died on us. John decided he preferred the fog.

Entering the first of the shipping lanes off Ushant, we could hear a big ship sounding its fog horn, one prolonged blast at 2 minute intervals. We searched under the forward bunk boards for our radar reflector, a large collapsible mesh type that we coupled up and hoisted. Perhaps the result was an echo on their radar screen as the ship's fog horn immediately changed to two prolonged blasts, meaning that they had stopped engines. Later, when south of the Lizard, we heard the unmistakable deep throated blast of a transatlantic liner travelling fast across our bow. We could see nothing, but some while after she passed, *Pintail* climbed a huge unbroken swell racing silently southwards. It was an unsettling experience in an otherwise smooth sea. We reached Falmouth in good order some forty hours out of Camaret, and a further 170 miles brought us back to Bosham.

Round Britain – the start

During the winter of 1963–4 *Pintail* was rigged as a yawl. A tiny mizzenmast was added which enabled us to hoist a large mesh radar reflector on the triatic stay between the two masts. The idea in 1964 was to sail round mainland Britain via the east coast of Ireland and back to Bosham. The voyage would have to be fitted in during limited holidays and weekends. We would leave *Pintail* at the nearest port when time ran out.

We set off for Salcombe on the first leg with three on board to be joined by Hugh at Salcombe for the passage to Falmouth. From there we sailed for Milford Haven, Pembrokeshire, first calling in at Mousehole for a night's rest and to allow the weather to moderate as we were committed to a haul of about 120 miles from Mousehole to the entrance of Milford Haven. This was across open water, bereft of bolt holes in the event of bad weather. After rounding Land's End, passing a mile to seaward of Longships lighthouse, we set off into northeasterly winds force 4. All day and all night *Pintail* pitched and thumped her way through a lumpy head sea. We worked four hour tricks at the helm, but off watch the forward berths under the cuddy were bumpy and noisy as *Pintail* fought her way northwards. This was the longest open water beat to windward she had faced, truly an uphill struggle.

Some thirty-eight hours later, we anchored off Dale inside the entrance to Milford Haven just before midnight. The estuary, attractive and interesting, was in its infancy as a major oil port. Next day we sailed up as far as Lawrenny, an enchanting unspoilt estuary with a small frowning castle. We returned to Dale where we laid her up for the winter.

During that winter my mother became desperately ill with

cancer. Her courage and will sustained her until January 1965 when she died. My father was absolutely wonderful at looking after her, as she insisted, quite rightly, on going home after an operation to arrest the cancer had failed. I went up to London as often and for as long as I could to help.

In April four of us including Hugh returned to Dale, camped on a hill and set to preparing *Pintail* for sea. Next month three of us set sail for Ireland departing St Ann's Head at the entrance to the Milford Haven estuary in very poor visibility. We set course to give the Smalls a wide berth, all thoughts of a short cut through the inner passage banished by the fog. A good 35 miles of the 70 mile passage was across St George's Channel, the southern entrance to the Irish Sea. This was completely open water and *Pintail* seemed very small. Her freeboard was low enough for us to lean over the side to do the washing up. However the sea was generally smooth, the breeze fretful and contrary as night fell. Passing the Tuskar Rock in the early hours the northerly wind increased suddenly, and the nearer we got to Rosslare the harder it blew. Now deeply reefed, *Pintail* bashed her way to windward lurching and heeling to the squalls. We were glad to reach harbour even though it gave little shelter in the northerly wind. Secured to a large buoy we endured a gale tossed day and night mostly in our berths as it was too rough to go ashore in the rubber dinghy. The next day we left *Pintail* afloat in the charge of the lifeboat coxswain. He insisted on inspecting *Pintail*'s carefully reinforced sampson post to which his mooring would be secured. Caution is the hallmark of seamen familiar with the forces generated by heavy weather in limited shelter. The coxswain satisfied, we caught a ferry to Fishguard and a train home.

Returning to Rosslare we sailed northwards inside the shallow offshore banks in relatively sheltered water. In the distance we could see the Wicklow mountains. As always when in sight of land, we repeatedly took bearings with the hand bearing compass to fix our position, as John was fanatical about keeping the navigation plot going. This had to be worked up from time, true course steered, leeway, log distance through the water and tidal streams. John maintained that safety in his small and open vessel depended upon accurate positioning so that dangers could be avoided and sensible courses shaped if the weather deteriorated. From Dun Laoghaire harbour with its massive stone piers built in Victorian times we took a taxi into Dublin to have a quick look at the great river Liffey and the old Georgian squares.

On 21 June we departed Dun Laoghaire in a strong southerly wind with no foresail or mizzen set and four rolls down on the mainsail. The weather worsened so we put into Howth four hours later and decided to stay the night there. Next morning we slipped in a rising southwesterly, three rolls down on the main, and by afternoon had reached Skerries, a small fishing harbour, which I loved. We moored alongside the fish boats whose friendly crews generously gave us enormous Dublin Bay prawns. It was a delightful place to be gale bound for four days. The seafarers there were interested in little *Pintail*'s voyaging. They judged her to be a proper yacht. We left on a calm evening under motor but the next day the wind rose as we passed inside South Rock lightvessel to Portavogie in Northern Ireland, 60 miles from Skerries. Exhausted, we set about putting up the cover and cooking a meal. Slipping later that evening after a nap, we sailed up the coast arriving in the early hours at the lovely working port of Donaghadee where we left *Pintail* to return home once more.

Leaving Donaghadee at 0730 hours on 9 July we sailed north northeast up the North Channel into the Firth of Clyde towards the tiny island of Ailsa Craig. The wind got up and lollopy seas made the setting of smaller headsails, often my job, extremely wet. John sailed into the lee of Ailsa Craig for a short respite from the rough sea running, but explosive gusts of wind off the crag repeatedly laid *Pintail* on her beam ends. We shot out from there quickly, the rough open water being preferable to those demonic blasts of wind. It was cold too, an intense, penetrating cold as night fell. Seated in the cockpit we stamped our feet, clapped hands and sang in an effort to keep warm. Finally, we sheltered in Lamlash Bay on the Isle of Arran at 2200 hours where it felt even colder as we dropped the hook. We set up the cover and lit the gas lamp and stove to get a fug up while cooking. Next morning after my quick swim, we set off for Rhu in the Gareloch where we left *Pintail*.

Two of us returned with Hugh and Geraldine for a perfect sail in wonderful scenery from Rhu through the Kyles of Bute and up Loch Fyne to Ardrishaig at the entrance to the Crinan Canal. The first lock was fairly nerve-racking as a large motor sailer with a vague skipper who made no effort to take up the slack on his lines was in danger of crushing us. After escaping from him, John decided to sail through the narrow canal. He managed this for most of the way with a lot of fast deck work every time we were headed. The children loved it; there were locks to be opened and the swans to be fed. We left *Pintail* at Crinan and returned home by train.

Three of us returned and set off for Oban leaving Luing to starboard and the dreaded Gulf of Corryvreckan between Jura and Scarba to port. We anchored off Luing for lunch and watched the seals. It was a sparkling day with blue sea and sky and green islands. Then we pressed on through Kerrera Sound to Oban where *Pintail* was laid up ashore in a lock-up garage.

Early in 1966 we fitted her out for the season. Launching *Pintail* down the harbour's steep ramp was an alarming exercise. She was so heavy when loaded that she nearly took off on her own in spite of trolley wheel chocks and restraining lines. All our protective instincts for this much loved vessel came to the fore as we struggled successfully to stop her.

That year we were unable to sail in *Pintail*, and John took her on by himself singlehanded from Oban to Lochinver on the Sutherland coast. Failing to find a suitable winter berth he sailed her back singlehanded to the Clyde where he laid her up in a garage at the Rhu post office. This had the advantage of being close to his relatives' house in Helensburgh which he could convert into a temporary dockyard for the boat's gear as was his wont.

7

Getting Qualified

In 1966 I started proceedings on legal aid against my husband in an uncontested divorce. In lieu of maintenance I had the house, Windrift in Bosham, as settlement, which is what I wanted. I was now living on my own except during the holidays when Hugh returned from school and Geraldine from college. The snag was that the house was mortgaged. I was untrained. How could I earn a living?

Swimming and diving and leaving school early had not helped. I could touch-type and had done some freelance work, but you have to be really fast to earn more than pin money, and anyway I disliked it. I had taken a shorthand course in 1962, but sixty words a minute was hardly fast, and the idea of being a secretary filled me with gloom and despondency. With all the emotional upheaval I was agitated and anxious about how we would survive.

Friends pressed me to apply for a job as matron or housekeeper at a boarding school, but I had no wish to live in and it would entail letting or selling the house, thus depriving the three of us of our roots. I did not like sewing, housekeeping or cooking although I got on with them, and fresh food and home cooking kept us healthy. With no obvious talent I decided that I must try for something that I really liked and could work hard at.

My cruising experience had given me a grounding in seamanship and sea sense and I was learning more navigation at evening class; but the instructor was erratic, did not prepare his work with care and seemed more interested in recounting stories than in teaching. If I wanted to earn a living from the sea I would have to find really top class tuition and go all out for a professional qualification. My research found the School of Navigation at Warsash, the College of Nautical Studies for Merchant Service officers, which was then part of Southampton University. I enrolled for the two evenings a week stipulated for the six month course required for the old Board of Trade Yacht Master (Coastal) certificate. The final papers for chartwork, navigation, world meteorology and magnetism and a three hour oral were the same as those taken by Merchant Service Masters and Mates. We were excused ship's loading, stability and law.

I flung myself into these studies, sitting quietly at the back of the class and working hard. The syllabus seemed daunting and the teaching was fast since it assumed a great deal of previous knowledge. From the first lesson I decided that I could either listen intently to the lectures or try to make hasty notes, including textbook references. My shorthand would have been too slow and I doubted whether I could decipher it afterwards so I scribbled staccato notes which I studied when I returned home. Large gaps in my formal education meant I had to work twice as hard to make up for my deficiencies, particularly in mathematics. We had to cover the whole of magnetometry and be able to adjust a ship's compass with soft and hard iron correctors. I flipped gloomily through the recommended textbook certain I would never understand it but determined to try, since without that knowledge I would be unable to pass the final examination. In the end I became so fascinated with the subject that I wanted to become a compass adjuster.

Hugh, then sixteen and at Charterhouse, was working for his A levels in pure and applied maths and physics. Realising how worried I was, he decided to help me with his own enthusiastic form of correspondence course in mathematics. Despite his own work problems, reams of the stuff arrived for me to struggle with, and I came to dread the post. In discussion with me in his holidays we alternated between total despair when I failed to grasp his modern maths (or any other maths for that matter) and hilarious laughter when by what he considered to be wildly unconventional methods, I arrived undaunted at the right answers.

I worked flat out from a standing start, disciplining myself to learn and understand quickly. The old 'rules of the road', the International Regulations for the Prevention of Collision at Sea, I learned by heart. Claude, the lurcher, must have learned them too as I recited out loud while walking him round the creek! I shut myself off from everyone bar the children while studying at Warsash. It was a marvellous place. Captain John Williams, Extra Master, who taught me several of the subjects, also skippered the large sailing vessel *Halcyon* which took full time Merchant Service cadets to sea for experience under sail. I found John Williams's expert tuition invaluable.

April 1967 was exam time at the Board of Trade examination centre on the fifth floor of South Western House in Southampton. On the first day we sat papers on magnetometry and meteorology, followed by chartwork and navigation on the second day, and signals, morse and semaphore on the third. I had already passed the Board of Trade eyesight and lantern test. My eyesight had always been excellent and I was not colour blind. However, the lantern test was literally a great eye opener. Two of us went in together to be examined.

It was pitch dark inside, and when my turn came to be tested I had to be guided to the high chair. As my eyes grew accustomed to the blackness I began to discern minute pinpricks of light. The examiner showed me each of the three colours to allow me to familiarise myself. The white light was yellowish like the old-fashioned oil lamps at sea, the green was whitish and the red, I am glad to say, looked red. I had to call out the colours as they came up rapidly two at a time from left to right. I found myself muttering under my breath 'the white's yellow and the green's white but the red is red', like some comedy film. My concentration was intense.

Signals had been taught at college by a former Yeoman of Signals. We had to be able to send and receive by flashing light at six words a minute and by semaphore at eight words a minute. We also had to know how to use the 1931 International Code of Signals which was more complicated than the revised 1969 edition. Morse by flashing light rather than by sound was a struggle as one stared blankly at the light without any rhythm. Semaphore was quickly learned and quickly forgotten if not regularly used. Our class had suggested to the Yeoman that we did better after a warm-up. This he took to heart and kindly arranged for those taking the exam to have a practice run at the Missions to Seamen building in Southampton before our test at South Western House. Certainly it worked for us and he said it was a practice he might continue with the cadets.

At the examination candidates of all nationalities sat in random pairs facing opposite ways, one to call out the letters and numbers signalled and one to write down. The use of the phonetic alphabet was essential to avoid confusion between, say, 'p' and 'b'; 'e', 'c' and 'd', particularly when callers were not English. The calling out was supposed to be done quietly but the air was filled with stage whispers, some right, some wrong.

My orals were held five days after the written examinations, which gave me a breathing space for more revision. Just before the exam the clerk to the Masters and Mates put his head round the door and said, 'you have passed everything well so far.' What a relief. That gave me the encouragement I needed for the orals.

First was Captain Beall's deviascope, set up to simulate the magnetic state of a steel ship. I had to swing the compass and work out both the strength of the magnets needed to correct it and the distance to insert them. There was a factory chimney outside the window from which to take bearings, but half way through swinging the compass on eight equidistant points, I was wooded by the bars of the window and could not see the chimney on that bearing. 'Keep calm, choose another chimney and start again', I told myself as I began all over again slowly and painstakingly to take accurate bearings. I calculated the coefficients by the long method on paper rather than using the shorter tentative method. I then inserted the right corrector magnets: soft iron spheres, Flinder's bar, fore and aft and athwartship's magnets and heeling error bucket with magnets according to my calculations. I swung the compass again to be certain that it had been corrected properly and the deviation eliminated. All was well. The examiner checked it, then waited for me to stow the magnets, presumably to ensure that I had put the opposite poles together to enable them to keep their magnetic properties.

Then it was off to another room for the rest of the orals: standing and running rigging, purchases and tackles, breeches buoy, bends, knots, splices and passing stoppers; handling of power boats (in theory) including transverse thrust; safety equipment; finding the sextant error; rules of the road; barometer with Gold slide and so on. I was examined by Captain Freeker who had a reputation for being fierce. I found him courteous and pleased with my results. When he told me I had passed out well, at first I just could not believe it; then I was so delighted I did not even mind being stuck in the overcrowded lift between floors on the way down.

8

Round Britain Completed

Pintail was still laid up in the Clyde and John wanted to complete her round Britain voyage so, exams over, I joined him. We again sailed through the Crinan Canal and up the Sound of Mull to Tobermory. Alarming gusts of wind generated by the mountains prevented us from cleating the main sheet which often had to be let fly to avoid a capsize. From Tobermory we sailed round Ardnamurchan Point with fair tide and wind, leaving Muck and Eigg to port. By nightfall in a rising southerly wind, with only a deeply reefed mainsail set, I was crouched beneath the cuddy with my torch trying to read the pilot book's directions for entering Mallaig. At that moment out of the gloom to port glided the lights of the local fishing fleet making for harbour. Delighted, John followed them into shelter where *Pintail* – still under a scrap of sail – made a fine job of beating through the crowded anchorage to a mooring near the weather shore. Here we were gale bound.

With a fair wind we tracked up the Sound of Sleat between Skye and the mainland and shot through the narrow Kyle Rhea with its 8 knot tidal streams at springs into Lochalsh. Through the Kyles we went and into Portree, capital of Skye, where we stopped for the night. Next day was a straight-forward roughish sail with a following wind to Lochinver on the Sutherland coast. We tied up to the fishing pier for a rest before rounding the Point of Stoer in a rising wind and rough water into the shelter of Eddrachillis Bay to Drumbeg. Here we were weatherbound for two days in a southerly gale. With the centreplate and drop rudder raised *Pintail*'s shallow draft enabled her to anchor close aboard the beach for the best shelter.

Directly the weather moderated we sailed northward. Outside Handa Island the fair wind and the fair tide began to fade and motoring now, we decided to put in to Kinlochbervie to await a favourable stream and to buy petrol, our last chance to refuel before tackling the north coast of Scotland. We made an evening departure towards Cape Wrath, the northwest corner of Sutherland. Sailing northwards we spoke to a small yacht sailing southwards and learned that she was out of Scullomie, Kyle of Tongue which her skipper recommended as a refuge. The wind was rising again, *Pintail* was accelerating and an hour or so after departure the shipping forecast was southerly force 7. Under a black cloud and in haste to reach the shelter of the windward shore, we rounded the Cape very close to and passed inside Dustic Rock, 7 cables northeast of Cape Wrath with the cliffs and lighthouse close aboard to starboard. Reaching now in a rising wind, fading light and lashing rain squalls we rushed eastwards along the north coast of Sutherland as close to the shore as we dared, hoping to reach Loch Eriboll some 40 miles out from Kinlochbervie before these offshore squalls overpowered us and blew us out to sea.

We found Loch Eriboll in the pitch darkness and with the motor on thumped our way in against the southerly wind gusting strongly. With difficulty we found Port Macon on the western side of the loch and anchored where indicated in the pilot book with the rocky shore seemingly close under our stern. Although the water was smooth, gusts of mighty gale force descended on us repeatedly and *Pintail* sailed around madly on her light anchor rope. As usual in the dark we appeared to be right on top of the land and anchor watch had to be mounted. When the day dawned the gusts were just as fearsome but the shore at least was much further astern than we had feared in the blackness of the night.

Two eighty-year-old retired ferrymen emerged from the only house on the shore, came down the jetty and waved, so we upped anchor and went alongside. One of the old boys gave us some of their fish which a trawler had just delivered and told us he had a home help who would shortly be arriving on her bike. We were amazed. It appeared deserted and miles from anywhere, with apparently only one other house and a telephone box, but the old chaps were clearly well looked after. On the ferrymen's suggestion and with their insistent, enthusiastic and expert help, we secured our nylon warp to the jetty and veered off to anchor with this safety line should the anchor drag. We remained weather bound all day with gale force gusts exploding down on *Pintail* from the mountains.

Next day we set out into the turbulent waters round Whiten Head and with a fair wind scudded along the coast in a rough and dangerous sea to the Kyle of Tongue where we found Scullomie hidden behind giant boulders on the eastern shore. This proved to be a deserted man-made harbour with an excellent stone built quay and bollards, where in contrast to the hazards of the open sea we lay in perfect shelter and warm sunshine. Next morning we sailed the 32 miles to Scrabster for fuel, stores and a new patent log rotator we had ordered. There we waited for the right tide to carry us through the Pentland Firth.

We made an evening departure to reach Dunnet Head at slack water, after which it would be downhill all the way eastwards towards Duncansby Head some 18 miles away. We passed the Men of Mey rocks before the race got too strong. The tide quickly picked up speed from slack to 7 knots, but the wind was light northerly on the beam as we left the Castle of Mey to starboard and the Old Man of Hoy in Orkney far away to port. Carried by the fierce tide we shot through the Pentland Firth taking the inner sound between Stroma and John O'Groats, rounded Duncansby Head and sailed down the east coast of Scotland past Wick. From there we set course across the Moray Firth to Kinnairds Head in smooth seas and light winds. Some 100 miles out from Scrabster we entered Fraserburgh harbour to await a fair tide and to replenish stores.

Leaving that evening we carried the fair tide round Rattray Head against a persistent headwind. Passing Peterhead after dark I shaped course for Bell Rock lighthouse at the mouth of the Firth of Tay while John slept. It was pitch black and every so often a wave splashed noisily alongside. With only a light breeze this surprised me. Then to my amazement I saw the tail of a large dolphin, porpoise or even whale keeping station with us and hoped that he would not thump *Pintail*'s slender planking. Eventually, much to my relief, he tired of his games and pushed off.

At dawn a fresh east southeasterly wind and a steep beam sea brought a wave aboard the cockpit. I was summoned from my berth urgently to plot a course for the nearest tenable port, which from study of the chart proved to be Stonehaven directly downwind. Navigation had to be accurate running down towards a rockbound lee shore at low water. Long and hard we stared ahead for a sight of the harbour entrance hidden somewhere among the distant granite cliffs. Eventually there it was dead ahead. In past the breakwater we hurtled, John still grumbling about his sea boots being full of water. The joke was that he went to sea in an open boat but hated getting wet. The chart table was a small board with an Admiralty chart folded and clipped to it. I navigated with parallel rules and dividers, with a torch between my teeth at night, bent double under the cuddy perched on the athwartship seat. It was a hard apprenticeship.

Leaving Stonehaven next day, a northerly wind carried us quickly southwards as far as Bell Rock where we were first becalmed and then headed. We struggled on through a misty night, and at dawn on track we rounded Longstone light on the Farne Islands off the Northumberland coast. After a landfall in thick weather outside Coquet Island lighthouse, some 20 miles further south, it was an all day beat against a southeasterly wind to Blyth, about 120 miles from Stonehaven, where we left *Pintail*.

We returned later with Hugh to sail southwards across the mouths of the Tyne and Wear, which had a good deal of shipping. The seasonal westerlies promised by the pilot book did not materialise. It was tack by tack all the way. We lay in the old coal dock at West Hartlepool for the night alongside the derelict machinery and in the morning tacked down the Yorkshire coast past Whitby and in and out of Robin Hood bay in a gigantic thunderstorm to reach Scarborough. An abortive start due to strong contrary winds took us round a pirate radio ship and back into port. After an evening restart we rounded Flamborough Head in a beautiful but sinister pink dawn and put in to Bridlington where again we left *Pintail*.

I was starting to get work so was unable to join her for the rest of the voyage. Richard Tetley shipped aboard as far as Harwich where he disembarked and John, at one with his beautifully balanced little yawl, sailed *Pintail* singlehanded back to Bosham, calling in at Ramsgate en route. A round voyage of some 2,000 nautical miles Bosham to Bosham had been completed.

My mother with Tootoo our
greyhound in Ma'adi desert

My parents James and Jess
Newman, my brother Derek and me
in our garden in Ma'adi, 1929

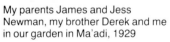

My father

The start of a flying 1½ forward somersault tucked from the 3 metre springboard at Breach Candy pool, Bombay, India, 1941

Back somersault straight from the 3 metre springboard at Breach Candy pool, Bombay, 1941

Reverse somersault (or full gagnor) in the tucked position from the 3 metre springboard at Breach Candy pool, Bombay, 1941

Reverse dive (or half gagnor) straight, from the 3 metre springboard at Breach Candy pool, Bombay, 1941

1½ forward somersault in the piked position from the 3 metre springboard at Breach Candy pool, Bombay, 1941

Cape Town, 1941

Ellis Park pool,
Johannesburg,
S.A., 1943

Swallow dive,
London, 1943

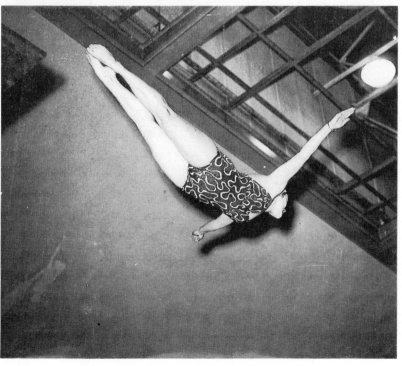

1948, The Olympic pool at Wembley. 10 metre highboard diving

1948 Olympic Games at Wembley

With Hugh, Geraldine and Claude No. 2 at Windrift, Bosham, 1961.
Copyright Chichester Observer

Pintail, 1960,
close hauled
under sloop rig
in Bosham
Channel.
Copyright
Chichester
Photographic
Service

Pintail, 1960,
alongside
Bosham quay
showing two
berths forward
and after
berths/seats.
Copyright
Chichester
Photographic
Service

Pintail, 1960, running before the wind.
Copyright Chichester Photographic Service

Pintail, 1960, on her mooring with harbour cover set up.
Copyright Chichester Photographic Service

Pintail, 1960, showing storage under berth boards and seats.
Copyright Chichester Photographic Service

Pintail, 1989,
reaching under
double headed yawl
rig.
Photograph Beken of
Cowes Ltd

Pintail, 1989,
showing the later
modifications

Pintail alongside
Flying Light at Cowes

John

Portisham under my command for the first time on the press day in Portsmouth Harbour, 1978.

On the bridge securing alongside Marlborough pier, press day 1978.
Copyright Daily Express

Press day on Marlborough pier.
Copyright Southern Newspapers, Southampton

In command, Navy Days Portsmouth. Trips round the harbour for the general public

On Portisham's bridge at Royal Clarence yard before departing for Ipswich

Head of Unit, Littlehampton, 1985

RNXS Littlehampton crew on board
Portisham at Royal Clarence yard,
1988

Chartwork on qualifying voyage to Gibraltar in Flying Light, 1987

Rough seas off
Portugal bound
for Gibraltar,
1987

Behind the wheel of Flying Light at Camper and Nicholson's marina, Gosport

A mast top view of Flying Light, 1988.
Copyright The Guardian

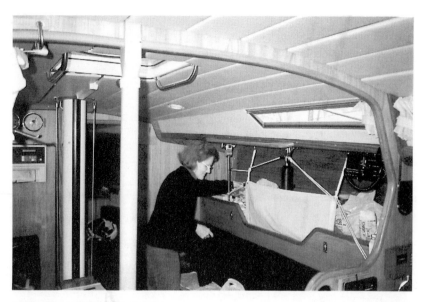

In the saloon, Flying Light, 1988

Busy at Plymouth with pre-race preparations, 1988

With Hugh and John, busy at Plymouth with pre-race preparations, 1988

More pre-race preparations, 1988

At Plymouth on Flying Light with, clockwise: Mrs Diana Downey, Hugh, Cdr Sir David Mackworth and John. In the background, the weatherfax showing a synoptic chart

Geraldine weaving the
foredeck safety net!

With Geraldine and the
present of a T-shirt from
Lady (Baba) Mackworth
(It says 'rough weather
cruising against the wind,
Long Island, New
York State.')

Evening before departure in the Plymouth marina café with, clockwise: Chris Dyer, Geraldine, John, Hugh, Brian Dawson and Jane Bilton

Flying Light approaching the transatlantic start line

Away at last – the adventure begins
Copyright Tony Byers, BBC SW

On track for the Eddystone Light
Copyright Tony Byers, BBC SW

Flying Light on her own
Copyright Tony Byers, BBC SW

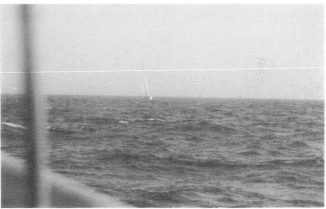

First sight of Flying Light from the Newport tow boat

Flying Light from the Newport tow boat

Is that the tow
boat?

Yes, it is

How lovely to
see you

Welcome back to Gosport. Left to right: TV crew, Air Vice Marshal Johnny Downey (Cruising Commodore Bosham Sailing Club), Jan Reid and Mrs Sheila Challis

The transatlantic crew reach home port

Welcome home from Hugh and Geraldine.
Copyright The News Centre, Hilsea, Portsmouth

Celebrations with Brian, John, Geraldine and Hugh

9

Jobs

My first professional job after returning from Bridlington was as skipper/navigator aboard a 35 foot Holman yawl, taking her owner and family for their summer cruise from Chichester harbour to the Channel Islands and the north Brittany coast. Strong tides, rocky shores and often indifferent visibility kept me working hard at the navigation. Morlaix was our furthest port of call.

My interest in becoming a compass adjustor meant two further years of practical training. I could not afford this and went to work at Emsworth Yacht Harbour starting in January 1968. It was a friendly informal place where I typed, learned accounting and where and how to buy stores both for the yard and for the chandlery shop, served yachts with fuel and generally ran about. It was all good experience.

A year later I passed the Board of Trade bridging examination in astronavigation. This included working out sun, moon and star sights, finding the deviation of the compass by time azimuth or by amplitude of a heavenly body, and the use of traverse tables to find one's position in latitude and longitude at any time given courses steered, distance run and tidal streams. Those of us who already had the old Yacht

Master (Coastal) certificate needed only to pass this extra astronavigation exam to qualify for the Board of Trade Yacht Master Ocean certificate.

I took on the job of delivering from the Solent to the east coast of Scotland, a brand new 37 foot glass fibre stern trawler built for research work. She had a single screw and was driven by a Perkins diesel which from experience I have found to be reliable. Since there were no sails, I needed an engineer as crew and John agreed to come. As she was a bare boat I had to take a lot of gear including safety equipment with us. Our passage took us up channel through the Gull Stream, across the Thames Estuary and up the east coast past Haisborough and Dudgeon lightvessels, where early on the third day we entered a very thick fog bank and immediately reduced speed. With no radar or electronic aids and an unreliable log, navigation was by estimated position only, using engine revolutions per minute (rpm) to assess our speed. Two hours later our next turning mark, the Dowsing lightvessel, suddenly became audible and just visible on the port bow some yards off, the powerful light hardly penetrating the fog.

We refuelled en route from spare drums of diesel we had taken on board to allow a non-stop voyage. Two hours past the Dowsing the engine died, surged rapidly and stopped again. Fuel lines were inspected for leaks on the suction side of the fuel pump but nothing major was found, and the engine was restarted successfully. By early afternoon, still in fog, we heard Flamborough Head diaphone off the port bow and turned sharply east to gain sea room from the lee shore as the engine was unreliable. The engine failed on seven separate occasions. We staggered on as best we could, but that evening as we tried to get under way for the eighth time, the starter motor exploded. With no means of starting the engine manually we were powerless. I had kept the estimated position going meticulously and now maintained a plot of the tidal drift as we drifted, using the echo sounder as an aid to fixing our position.

After twenty hours of fog, the visibility improved for just long enough to sight the Filey buoy flashing abeam and to confirm the plot. At 0300, after drifting for eight hours, our estimated position coincided with the 20 fathom depth line, and we let go the anchor and paid out all 100 fathoms of warp. This held well in the strong tidal stream. Two hours later a fishing vessel passed across our bow. I signalled repeatedly code letter F – Foxtrot by morse lamp, meaning 'I am disabled, communicate with me', and they turned and offered us a tow. I asked their terms and they said we could discuss it in harbour. Without power we could not recover the anchor by hand so we bent their rope on our anchor warp and they brought it in. We entered Scarborough harbour under tow at 0630 hours after a passage of 350 miles. Mr Pasby, the skipper of the fishing vessel, would accept no recompense, so all we could do was buy him a crate of beer. The fishermen, incredibly kind and helpful, took the attitude, 'your turn today, maybe ours tomorrow'. As the engine would take time to fix, we returned that afternoon to London, exhausted after sleeping so little during the three day voyage.

Ten days later we set out again. With tanks full and smooth water all started well, but early next morning we encountered a small beam sea and soon after the engine stopped. The third time this happened it dawned on us that there was a correlation between roll of vessel to a beam sea and engine stoppage. After the third breakdown, the new starter expired, and we were left derelict once more with the Farne Islands about three miles off the port bow. We sent up rocket parachute flares and, as we drifted nearer to the Farne Island rocks, orange smoke flares. The anchor was ready for let go. A local fishing boat closed us, the skipper reporting that the Seahouses lifeboat was on her way and that he would stand by us until she arrived. This time the RNLI was involved in salvaging a commercial vessel, so the Board of Trade had to be called in to inspect the trawler and report.

The cause of the engine failure turned out to be the installation of two shallow fuel tanks, one on each beam. When the vessel rolled beyond a certain angle, the suction pipe in the tank on the high side was exposed, causing air to be sucked in. When the air reached the fuel injectors, the engine stopped. The starter motor failure could have been due to overcapacity of battery for engine starting. The Board of Trade insisted on the installation of a centre tank. I refused to take the vessel any further.

10

Family Independence

That was a lean time trying to make ends meet on a small salary at the yacht harbour with no financial reserves. Only the interest on the house mortgage had ever been paid. The capital owing had remained at the same figure as when it was built, and now I was asked to begin paying off both capital and interest. Unable to foresee the future I had to hang on to the house as a base for the three of us. There was little time for sailing as a job. I had to paint the inside of the house again during weekends and evenings. Outside nothing had been touched since it was built and it was slowly rotting away.

I was concerned about my father who wanted to stay put after my mother died. He came to stay for weekends and longer, we saw him in London and telephoned him regularly. Where Geraldine and Hugh were concerned I felt strongly, given my own experience, that they should be well educated. Neither objected. In 1963 Hugh had been awarded a bursary to Charterhouse, one of the first schools to teach his subject, modern mathematics. A natural athlete, he was Victor Ludorum at his prep school and at Charterhouse was captain of cross-country running.

Geraldine passed A levels in geography, zoology and art

in 1964 and was determined to paint. She was accepted at Goldsmiths for her pre-diploma year, but despite having longed to go up to London she found it lonely and restricting – no fields, no water, no animals. Deciding after her pre-diploma year that painting was not for her, she chose to study woven textiles for her three year Diploma of Art and Design at Farnham (which later became the West Surrey College of Art and Design). After getting her degree Geraldine travelled to Iran with two girls who were students of ceramics, to examine Persian textiles and architecture. On her return she wanted to set up her own workshop, but with no income she accepted an offer to look after a family of four children for a year in Devon with time off for her own work. She set up her six foot loom in her bedroom and that started her off. Later Jo found an unfurnished hilltop cottage to rent for one pound a week in isolated country several miles from Bosham where she set up a luxury business of fine handwoven cloth in pure silk and cashmere. Some months later Farnham, her old college, offered her a part time job teaching history of textiles which enabled her to survive – just.

In 1967 Hugh passed pure and applied maths and physics at A level, took his university entrance in November and was accepted by Oxford to read physics. He was first awarded an exhibition and then at the end of the first year an open scholarship. After his degree he had a break from study before going to Leeds University to work for his PhD in solid state chemistry.

One Christmas we all felt overworked and scraped together enough cash to have a holiday. We booked a package trip to Djerba, Tunisia for a few days in the sun. Pop, then eighty-two, insisted we went without him. I insisted that he should go for his inoculations. Oh no, he said gloomily, he definitely would not. He would only be a nuisance. Next day he rang up. His passport was ready, the doctor did not consider inoculations were for him at his age and he was already packed. It was winter but the open air pool was sheltered and sunny. Without a thought Pop dived in and tried under water to lift me up on his shoulders as he had so often in my youth. Unable to manage it, he surfaced; 'must be getting old,' he complained! Eight days after his eighty-ninth birthday in 1980 he died following a short illness. His independent spirit had kept him going wonderfully well and I missed him greatly.

In 1970 John and I decided to sail *Pintail* to Lundy Island, off the coast of North Devon, some 300 miles from Bosham. We called in at Mousehole, Cornwall, departing the next morning before dawn in what seemed a light offshore breeze bound for the Scilly Isles on a west going tide. Out of the shelter of the land we soon realised there was far more weight in the wind than we had thought. Quickly we reefed *Pintail* and with six rolls of mainsail on the boom and the peak of the sail down to intermediate shroud level, we scorched westwards before a blistering wind. Day dawned gloomily with poor visibility. If we missed the rock strewn Scillies, the next stop was likely to be America! Accurate navigation was vital.

We decided to run down to Wolf Rock lighthouse and take a departure from there, but the rough water round it was too confused and dangerous for the little vessel so we sheered away westwards. *Pintail* ran under reefed main and no fore-sail, John steering mostly standing up with the tiller between his legs. I concentrated on the navigation until, after some anxious hours, St Mary's, the largest of the Scillies, appeared fine on our starboard bow just where it should have been. Next day we sailed to Tresco across the flats, to lie off New Grimsby pier. The flats are drying banks with heights above chart datum, which necessitated sailing at the right time on a rising tide. Tresco was enchanting, its vegetation tropical in parts.

A few days later we sailed northwest to clear Tresco leaving Round Island lighthouse to starboard and then 100 miles northeast to Lundy. This was open sea work for *Pintail* with no safe harbours should the weather worsen. It was calm as we sailed through the night watching the lights of a Shackleton Coastal Command aircraft which was circling to the north. Then it locked on a course straight for us; the roar of its engines growing ever louder and louder. Night was transformed into day as a stick of parachute flares floated down while the aircraft thundered over us; exciting entertainment for the long night watch. One flare hit the sea alongside us, making me jump and temporarily destroying our night vision. Next day the visibility deteriorated markedly and we could hear the southeast Lundy lighthouse fog signal which unexpectedly stopped. When we visited the lighthouse the keeper explained that his local visibility had exceeded one mile at that time.

Lundy's anchorage and main landing place were on the east side of the island, sheltered from the prevailing southwesterlies but open to easterlies. Having anchored *Pintail* on her heavy fisherman's anchor with two fathoms of chain attached to a long nylon rope, we landed on the beach in our rubber dinghy and climbed to the island's high plateau stretching some two and a half miles by half a mile. It was a lovely place full of wild life. We walked the length of Lundy to visit both lighthouses. The northern light consisted of a paraffin wick lamp magnified by an enormous nineteenth-century prism set in a bath of mercury to reduce friction when turning. The rotation of the light to create its particular characteristic was effected by a grandfather-clock-type ratchet and counterweight which had to be wound up manually every day. The southeast light was a small modern prism worked by electricity with an electric light bulb magnified.

We rode out a southwesterly gale in our Lundy anchorage,

then wasted no time in setting off for home as soon as the weather moderated, for this was no place to hang about. Again we had to traverse the dangerous north coast of Cornwall before rounding Land's End and the Lizard to regain the comparative safety of the south Devon coast with its deep water harbours.

A later voyage in *Pintail* took us westwards to Fowey, Falmouth harbour and back to the River Yealm where we were gale bound and running short of time. The wind had abated temporarily to a southwesterly force 4 but we had to leave. Across Lyme Bay it rose to force 5–6 and by the time we were five miles off Portland Bill to clear the race it had increased to 6–7 with a large following sea. With only the main up and that reefed down nine rolls, John turned northwards when we were past the Bill to get into the shelter of the race off Portland Bill. His theory was that this tidal race would break up the rough channel wave pattern and that downwind of it the sea would be smoother and safer. His theory proved correct. In the shelter of this natural breakwater we skirted the Shambles Bank, gained the lee of the Bill itself, and closed the coast near Lulworth Cove. Then we turned eastwards to take the inner pasage at St Albans Head instead of staying several miles off to clear the overfalls. This was a rough non-stop voyage for *Pintail*, scorching along day and night with the following sea giving her a roller-coaster ride, lifting her up on the crests and dumping her down into the troughs. 'Don't look aft' is the watchword in such conditions, as sight of the breakers brimming up astern can be unnerving!

I complained about the lack of hot food and drinks as cooking became impossible. The rougher the weather, the tougher the voyage and the greater the resort to dry biscuit. Even replenishing the ready use water bottle involved a major operation to reach the cans under the forward berths.

The following winter, *Pintail* became a doubled headed

yawl with a new and taller mizzenmast, a longer bowsprit to enable her to have a roller furling foresail and an inner forestay on which to set a staysail. Foam cushions similar to those on the cockpit seats replaced the lilos on the forward berths, and a new Sestral compass was mounted on a cockpit pedestal where a new main sheet jamming cleat was also located. John designed and had made two stainless steel water tanks to fit into the shallow bilges, with two fresh water pumps to give us instant access to water. He also designed stainless steel gimbals for the *gaz* stove and fiddles to take a pressure cooker. This was installed just under the canvas cuddy on the port side and could be used in all weathers without fear of hot spillage or flame out. A stern bracket was added to take the outboard motor where it remained permanently stowed. There were to be no more dangerous balancing acts.

11

RNXS

From a naval friend I heard of the Royal Naval Auxiliary
Service (RNXS), the only service to accept women for seagoing duties, and joined immediately in April 1970.

The RNXS evolved from the Royal Naval Minewatching
Service. It is a voluntary organisation formed in 1962 in support of the Royal Navy in the event of tension, emergency or
war, and provides seventy-five units and some 3000 trained
reserves ashore and afloat in the British Isles. The shorebased
arm is responsible for communications and control operations
in UK ports, while the seagoing part serves anywhere in home
waters. In 1964 the RNXS was allocated the first batch of
Ham class inshore minesweepers to support the Naval Control
of Shipping (NCS) organisation in the anchorage of shipping
and the assembly of convoys by acting as the link between
the ships and the shore. Unpaid part time civilians, uniformed
and administered by the Royal Navy, constitute this non-
combatant service, which afloat is subject to the Merchant
Shipping Act but not to the Naval Discipline Act, except in
war. The upper age limit is sixty afloat and sixty-five shorebased. The ranks are: qualified Naval Auxiliaryman, Leading
Naval Auxiliaryman and Chief Naval Auxiliaryman, which

last is the rank held by ships' skippers and charge engineers. Heads of units become Auxiliary Officers.

I joined Portsmouth unit, and we went to sea in the Ham class ex-inshore minesweeper *Portisham*. Her black hull was constructed of double skin diagonal planked timber sur-mounted by a grey non-magnetic aluminium alloy superstruc-ture with lattice mast and open bridge. Her dimensions were length 108 feet (33 metres), beam 22 feet, draught 7 feet; and she was powered by two 350hp Paxman diesels unblown and two Foden generators. She carried 4000 gallons (15 tons) of diesel fuel and 720 gallons of water.

Portisham was divided into compartments separated by closed bulkheads which made it impossible to walk through the ship below decks. Access to each compartment was by vertical companionway. There were eight bunks in the for-ward mess, two four-berth cabins aft, of which one was for women, heads and basins but no mod cons like showers. The sweeps and their machinery had been removed and the resultant space converted into a midships mess with eleven more bunks. Below decks were a galley, mess deck, radio room and engine room. From the mess deck right forward, a companionway led up and aft to the charthouse and up again to the open bridge where there was the skipper's chair, wheel, engine controls, VHF, standard compass binnacle and mag-netic steering compass. We used an Admiralty Gyro Magnetic Compass (AGMC), which is a magnetic compass assisted and stabilised by a gyro.

Each RNXS unit was allocated time for sea training by day, at weekends or for a week's cruise. Best of all was joining NATO exercises. The crew comprised skipper, mate, charge engineer, communicator, seamen and engineers. The unit to which the ship was allocated, victualled and prepared her for sea and cleaned ship after the voyage, leaving her ready for use by the next unit.

I joined ship for a voyage from Portsmouth to Grimsby, my first experience of passage making on board *Portisham*. We arrived in the Humber in the dark one morning to pick up a mooring buoy and secure until dawn. The volunteer leapt on to the buoy to pass a rope through the ring and bring it back on board but the skipper was unable to hold the ship alongside long enough, had to back off, turn and try again. I was astonished. I was told to train an Aldis lamp on this not-so-young crewman as he balanced precariously on the buoy bobbing about in the choppy sea in pitch dark and fine rain. However, all went well and eventually he scrambled aboard, not a bit put out by his experience.

In 1975 we sailed to Hull putting in at Chatham en route for Navy Days. We ran trips round the harbour for the general public, which was good fun. We were supposed to exercise with a helicopter in the Humber but it did not show, to my disappointment, as I had hoped for a ride. Then as we reached the open sea it arrived with time enough to hoist only one crew. 'Oh, for goodness' sake, take Denise,' said the Skipper. 'She's been pestering me ever since she heard.' It was freezing cold for May and I had on my polo-necked submariner's sweater and sea boots. Up I went in the strop, arms at my side in case I slipped out and with instructions from a helicopter crewman left on deck that I should on no account help myself. After I reached the open doorway of the cabin, the helicopter banked. Automatically I scrabbled for something to hold on to and stuck out my feet to brace myself, forgetting I was still attached to the wire. This produced much laughter and gesticulating from the winchman, as it was much too noisy to speak. I could just see the pilot's look of concentration and the coordinated interplay of hands and feet. They landed me impeccably between after winch and stern with a hefty pat on the back from the crewman to earth the static electricity generated by the rotor blades.

In August 1975 I caught a train to Chatham to join *Shipham*, *Portisham*'s sister ship, for my six-day mate's examination. Two years earlier I had transferred to the Littlehampton unit which had just formed a seagoing side to their shorebased section.

The theoretical part of the examination for mate took place ashore next morning, before our two day exercise in the Thames Estuary. As Officer of the Watch I was to take the ship from Tongue lightvessel through North Edinburgh channel, Knob channel and Oaze deep to Medway buoy, some 21 miles, giving estimated times of arrival at each buoy, having worked out track and speed over the ground taking tidal streams into account. There was a maze of buoyed channels through the sands. Next day was foggy, and by request we took stores out to Tongue lightvessel and sent them over by line. The fog horn at close quarters was deafening. How the lightvessel crew stood it for long periods without wearing their ear defenders, I could not imagine. Then with crews from other units we crossed the channel to Ostend. There was usually at least one joker on board. I had joined three hefty bearded crew members to line the decks as we entered Ostend harbour, when a slight clean-shaven latecomer dashed to fall in with us. 'Only beards and boobs allowed here,' shouted the joker. We entered harbour buckling at the knees. I passed out as Mate in the RNXS.

12

Sea Work

Back in October 1970 I decided the time had come to leave Emsworth Yacht Harbour to start on my own as a professional sailor. I started teaching navigation at the local college evening classes, although teaching had never appealed to me. However, I set my mind to it, and at least I knew the pitfalls from a student's point of view. The change from taking notes to being out in front was salutary. There was no give and take with large classes until a bolder one, often a woman, started to ask questions and broke the ice. As I became more experienced the ice broke more quickly. I taught beginners and advanced students both coastal navigation and astronavigation for three years between September and April each year. In 1971 I was elected a member of the Royal Institute of Navigation. Occasionally I taught navigation and seamanship privately at home and I delivered yachts or shipped aboard owners' vessels as skipper/navigator, but financially it was all rather fragile.

Yacht deliveries were interesting and demanding but hard going, as usually they needed to be non-stop and fast to make them pay. Finding even one crew was difficult; there were many volunteers but they were seldom free when required, and I often had to recruit a stranger who had little experience. I quoted realistic prices for transatlantic deliveries, one to Montevideo (6000 miles) and one to New York via the Azores, about 3,700 miles, but did not get them.

It was difficult to cost a delivery. With the owner on board as crew the charge was a daily rate. If he was not on board it had to be a lump sum based on distance and weather, the cost of victualling, buying charts and crew expenses. Net travelling costs to or from the vessel were extra, although I charged no travelling time. Effort had to be spent in agreeing the delivery arrangements before the start. If the vessel was lying locally I would check through its seaworthiness to the best of my ability and list navigation, safety and other equipment to bring with me, if it was not already aboard. My aim was to make everything clear to the owner beforehand so that he found the vessel at the destination looking exactly as he had last seen it, clean, undamaged and with no 'ifs or buts' or 'sorry, you owe me more money for this and that'. The exceptions were malfunctions or breakages on the vessel not caused by me. My own check-list of equipment was always sent to the owner to tick off and return. Some inexperienced owners thought if the vessel was plush below decks that was all that was required, never mind if the compass had not been swung! Experienced owners who hired me because they were short of time were the best, as their yachts were usually very well found. The worst deliveries were often brand new bare boats straight from the boatyard before owners had fitted them out. A great deal of basic gear had to be taken, even rags for cleaning ship when I reached the destination. The logistics of humping gear to and from the vessel were the worst, whether by bus, taxi, train or plane. My car would have been in the wrong place, and my business consisted of just me. At sea in command, sleep was short, so on completion I slept anywhere, anyhow, on station platforms, in trains or in the luggage compartment if I had too much gear for the carriage.

One problematic delivery was from the Clyde to the Thames Estuary. The owner had bought a secondhand 38 foot yacht through a shipyard. There was a rail strike so I had to fly to Scotland with an engineer as this was a twin screw motor vessel, a trawler type hull with steadying sail and a cruising speed of 6–7 knots. The problem was to assess what gear was missing from the vessel and take it with me. On the telephone I discussed the state of the yacht with the shipyard. The owner agreed a list of spares and rope that I needed on board, and the yard was asked to fuel the vessel, fill the water tanks and service the engine since the yacht had been out of commission for a year or more. All was agreed and confirmed in writing.

When we arrived on Saturday morning nothing had been done and the boatyard was due to close at noon. We found a shop prepared to deliver our food stores while the yard hastily set to work on the vessel, which was moored some way out. I took her on engine trials with the manager and his staff before setting out on a journey of nearly 1000 miles. 'Oh, that's nothing,' they said airily when one engine stopped. On the contrary, diesels do not stop unless something is wrong. When the second engine faltered I anchored the vessel to prevent them from getting ashore and leaving us kicking our heels until Monday. The yard now had to bleed both engines and drain off the water in the bottom of the fuel tank.

We finally set off from the Clyde at noon on Sunday. The weather brewed up en route with severe gale force 9 forecast. After a night passage we put into Stranraer harbour to find our water supply, which we had barely used, was exhausted. There had been no way of checking how much the tank held before setting off, as there was no dipstick. Clearly the yard had not bothered to fill her as promised. Alongside Stranraer quay there was no hose for yachts and we had none on board, so up and down the long ladder at low tide we went with bucket after bucket of water. Unable to remain alongside because of incoming ferries and ships we anchored in Wig, Loch Ryan at 0730 hours Monday to ride out the northwesterly storm.

When the wind moderated I decided to set course across the Irish Sea to Dun Laoghaire harbour, the weather shore, rather than go down the English coast. We reached Dun Laoghaire thirteen hours later to find no diesel there, which we needed for the next part of our long voyage. Only one road tanker was available then to refuel the fishing vessels; it serviced other ports as well and was working elsewhere. Until midnight I was telephoning one pub after another chasing someone I was told to contact. It proved impossible to feed an Irish telephone box without cutting oneself off. This complicated the proceedings. Eventually I spoke to a man who undertook to drop a note through a friend's door when he went to work early in the morning; this friend, he promised, would surely arrange for fuel to be available at Howth 10 miles north that same morning. This meant backtracking the vessel to Howth with no guarantee of supply when we got there. However, this shaky plan worked perfectly. The diesel was very cheap too, but we had to pay for the water we also needed!

We departed Howth on Wednesday morning and ran down the Irish coast past Tuskar Rock bound for Land's End, crossing the busy shipping lanes of St George's Channel in darkness. Surrounded by ships' lights, we gave way to those on our starboard side, but in the rough sea prevailing, the 'give way' vessels neither noticed nor cared about avoiding us, so when necessary we had to alter course for them also. Taking repeated bearings of the lights with the hand compass identified those ships threatening collision, and when the bearings remained constant we took evasive action. Rounding Land's End we made our way eastwards to the Isle of Wight for a fuel stop. As we were too early for a favourable tidal stream in the Needles channel, we anchored in Swanage Bay for a much needed nap, my first one since leaving Howth forty-four hours previously. Two hours later it was up anchor and on our way again to secure alongside Yarmouth quay for fuel, food and more sleep. By afternoon we had slipped our moorings and were proceeding up channel to the Dover Straits, past North Foreland, across the Thames Estuary at low water after another sleepless night, to reach Burnham-on-Crouch safely on Saturday afternoon after a 950 mile voyage. We scrubbed out, checked all was secure, telephoned the owner to advise him, ordered a taxi to the nearest station and staggered homewards by public transport humping the gear.

Another delivery I made was of a 36 foot ketch from Chichester harbour to Dartmouth, a distance of about 115 miles indicating a voyage normally of some twenty-four hours, but less with a following wind. It was March, when the low pressure systems came in fast often without the twenty-four hour ridge of high pressure that normally separates them in summer. Unseasonally the pressure had been high for several weeks giving calm weather, the intensity of the high holding back or diverting the lows away from our area. A week earlier I had delivered a new 30 foot yacht the 170 miles from Chichester harbour to Falmouth, in calm and thick fog all the way. Now the high was starting to subside and a string of lows out in the Atlantic was threatening. Departure day was calm, the journey short, deliveries had to press on and crew return to work, but I was unhappy about the weather pattern and telephoned the weather centre to ask the forecasting officer's opinion. He thought the first low was slow moving and the wind unlikely to exceed force 4 possibly 5 during the next twenty-four hours. Still uneasy, we departed Chichester harbour in a calm. The wind increased to southerly force 4 then veered southwest 5–6 and by midnight, when six miles south of Portland Bill, the wind veered again to northwest force 6–8. Reefed right down we were battling to windward in rough seas, and by dawn, under storm jib only, we were labouring in a severe gale northwest force 9. The sole crew member had succumbed to the motion and could not be roused from his berth. In the strong head sea running, I could not make to windward across Lyme Bay under storm jib alone and had found no trysail on board. I could heave to or run off up channel, but I was now singlehanded and aware of my own limits of endurance should the gales continue.

I decided to use the auxiliary engine. To prevent the bow falling off as she climbed up the enormous seas, I had to open the engine throttle to keep her head to wind until she was over the top of each roller-coaster wave. By heading the northwesterly wind into Lyme Bay I was moving towards the safety of a weather shore, where I could then hoist more sail and run down to Dartmouth. As she had to be helped over the rollers I was unable to leave the wheel, so stayed put in the open cockpit for hours sustained by a couple of pies and some fizzy lemonade. Still the crew was unwakeable. Early in the afternoon the wind backed to the west and my plan to gain the shelter of the weather shore now took me more directly towards Dartmouth. The tidal stream then turned in my favour and set us down in the right direction, but two miles off the Dartmouth entrance the stream turned contrary and I could barely stem the strong wind and tide. Although now in the lee of the land the rough sea persisted. Finally I made the entrance and reached Dartmouth marina, thirty-four hours out of Chichester. My face was snow white, caked with salt spray but the vessel was safely delivered.

Next day we took her right up river in ferocious winds to

her mooring among the drying banks at low water. The harbour master valiantly helped us both moor her. There was no pilot buoy to pick up, and the crew had difficulty in reaching down to pass a warp through the buoy ring and secure it back on board as the gusts blew the bow off once the way was off the vessel. The harbour master took us ashore in his launch, since we could not have rowed our rubber dinghy back and forth in that wind with so much gear. He gave us a lift to the station, saying he enjoyed helping us as it made a change from his usual routine.

I took on the delivery of a 28 foot Bermudan sloop with owner and wife as crew. The voyage was from Hoo marina on the Medway to Chichester, about 160 miles. Both crew had been students at my beginners' evening classes and now wished to collect their recently acquired secondhand yacht and put their training into practice on passage. Her draught meant we could only clear the mud flats at high water springs and negotiate the Kent coast inner passage on a falling tide as well. With the gloomy weather it would have been all too easy to run aground. Once clear of the channel, the propeller picked up a rope off Margate. There was nothing else for it but to go over the side. The weather was calm but the water was cold and a swell was running. For safety I attached the knife to a line from the boat in case I dropped it. I found it difficult, while sawing the rope away, to stay deep enough to keep the swell from crashing hull and propeller down on my head. After we had weathered North Foreland the wind increased against the swell, making for rough conditions. From then on it was headwinds all the way. When at last we reached Chichester harbour it was too rough and shallow to clear the bar, so we pressed on to Portsmouth's deep water.

Generally owners and their families have made me very welcome, but sometimes I have been regarded initially with suspicion, especially by strangers. I would tactfully check the yacht and equipment and insist that they borrow or buy any gear I considered essential. I also planned the passage before departure. To anyone inexperienced and with perhaps only a shortish voyage ahead, this seemed an unnecessary pre-caution. However, if the weather worsened suddenly en route they quickly came to understand the reasons for my prepara-tory work, and that gave them confidence in me. I always checked the steering compass even if it had recently been swung professionally and a deviation card provided. Some owners, of course, looked at me as if I were potty.

This routine paid off on one occasion. When I checked the compass which was taking us across the channel to France, I found it had 15° of westerly deviation which meant 15 miles out for every 60 miles sailed. Had the visibility closed down, we could be in jeopardy. Although the owner was inexperi-enced he had taken advice, the yacht was well found and the compass had been professionally swung, so he found it diffi-cult to believe anything was wrong. I looked around for any ferrous metal near the compass and discovered that various instruments had been added after the compass had been swung. Some could be removed which then left an easterly deviation of five degrees which I allowed for when plotting courses. I shipped aboard only for the outward bound voyage as the owner would be returning with friends some weeks later. I urged him to have the compass swung again before going on, as deviation changes with the ship's head; when he returned to England the five degrees east he experienced on a southerly heading would change to five degrees west on a northerly one, leaving them five miles out for every 60 miles travelled; that was exactly what happened, they told me later.

On another occasion an owner had ordered a new 40 foot ferrocement ketch. When it was supposed to be ready I was hired to take the owner and his wife cruising off the French coast for a month. It was agreed I would buy the necessary

94

Admiralty charts and publications on their behalf. I arrived at the yard to find the compass was to be swung that day. The owner did not realise the steel mesh in the concrete affected the compass nor that his hand bearing compass would prove useless. I pressed him to buy a Sestrel Moore compass with sight vane to mount on the coach roof giving an all round view. This could be checked for deviation separately from the steering compass which was mounted on a binnacle by the wheel and unsuitably positioned for taking bearings. Delivery of the yacht was apparently long overdue and I could not take over as skipper until first Lloyds had passed it as AI and secondly the owner had paid off the yard. Until then, the boatbuilder, who did not employ me, was technically the owner.

For the shakedown trials the builder proposed bringing his wife, two young sons and a friend to make a night passage to the Scillies into the teeth of a strong southwesterly. I had no wish to sail in such circumstances, expressed my objections and was overruled. I considered trials by night unnecessarily hazardous. Apart from the difficulty of assessing performance, if anything serious failed in an untried yacht it would not be easy to identify and rectify in a rough sea in the dark. I refused to go and the owner decided against it.

I suggested a short sail the next morning instead, weather permitting. Although the winds were strong they insisted on setting out with the boatbuilder in charge. Still unhappy, I was sent below to navigate. Various things broke including the topping lift attachment holding up a heavy wooden boom. Before the sails were hoisted it fell, injuring the finger of the builder's wife. He insisted on sailing despite the mounting shambles on deck and the young boys feeling sick and miserable in such a turbulent sea. Finally, my opinion was asked and we turned back.

A day or two later, under some arrangement without the

builder, we sailed towards Salcombe for the new engine check. I kept the estimated position going and fixed the position of the vessel regularly. 'Why do you keep fixing our position?' asked the owner. 'I can see the land, you can see the land, why the fuss?' 'Visibility can often close down quickly,' I replied tactfully. 'Oh yes,' came the retort somewhat mockingly. Thirty minutes later it did, and I had to enter Fowey in thick fog avoiding the rocks which would have been difficult had I not known where we were to start with. Dead silence until we had moored to a buoy. 'Denise, I see now why you keep fixing.'

Next day with strengthening winds we put into Plymouth. As we motored in the engine sounded most peculiar. Local engineers reported that the engine bed bolts had sheered and that the propeller shafts had probably not been aligned when installed. As nothing could be done there, we had to sail to Salcombe. I sailed the vessel in on the leading marks and the owner was horrified that we were not in dead centre channel. I explained. He was quick to learn if he saw it made sense and took over from me staying on the transit with fanatical accuracy. I was winning him over at last. The engine had to be taken out, a long job as it had been glassed in against the owner's instructions. Sadly, the voyage had to be abandoned.

13

My Own School

In 1973 responsibility for the Board of Trade Yacht Master examinations was taken over by the Royal Yachting Association (RYA) and the content redesigned specifically for yachtsmen. I telephoned the RYA rather gloomily to ask about the syllabus, and Lieutenant Commander Bill Anderson said he was to examine forty people to get the scheme off the ground. Would I like to go on a six day course to become – if successful – a RYA examiner? The course, out of Plymouth, was aboard the Nautical College's 90 foot gaff rigged ketch. As there were no winches, tackles had to be clapped on everything. She was heavy to get going, needed strong winds and manoeuvred poorly under engine. There were eleven candidates, mostly former Merchant Service masters, plus Bill Anderson as examiner.

Split into watches we each acted as skipper for half a day. It was an interesting course covering navigation, seamanship, boat handling and emergencies. My training in the RNXS was of help when I brought the vessel to a large mooring buoy. I walked forward to get a better view while giving the spoken helm and engine orders. To my relief I passed the course and was now on call from the local examination centre at Warsash to examine candidates for the RYA yachtmaster certificate.

Then quite suddenly I decided to start my own evening classes in navigation and seamanship. The instinct was so strong I knew it had to work, even if I had no money, no premises and only two weeks to advertise before colleges opened in September.

I tramped the streets of Chichester looking for a large unused hall and on recommendation tried a Chichester association which had a ground floor room used only occasionally. They agreed but wanted five pounds per evening which hardly seemed viable, as I intended charging only six pounds per person for the two terms as did the colleges run by the local authorities. If enough students joined that first year, and I ran really good courses, I might be able to use my track record to raise the fees subsequently. The association offered to take half of what I made that winter, win or lose. In the event seventy-nine people joined from a standing start, but at that level of charges I was going to be pretty hungry that winter!

I offered RYA courses for Beginners, Yachtmaster Offshore and Ocean shorebased certificates. Later on the beginner grades changed to Competent Crew and Day Skipper/Watch Leader, and a Coastal Skipper certificate was introduced. I bought a few extra trestle-type tables and some anglepoise lamps to supplement the room lights. Classes began on four evenings a week. The gear had to be brought to and from home each evening to leave the room clear for my landlord's use next day.

I bought cheaply twenty out of date Admiralty tide tables of a particular year and a similar number of out of date Nautical Almanacs for the astronavigation, on which to set my own exercises. These I lent out in class, which meant that I would not have to update my own exercises each year and would thus save much work. Later on the RYA issued their own dateless tables for classwork, a great improvement. Power cuts during that first winter of 1973 reduced the four evenings to three, but I was allowed to have the room in the afternoons for those who were free to come then. Luckily enough students could switch to the afternoons, but arranging it all was a lot of extra work.

In 1974 I had to hunt for another room as the Association was moving and eventually found a nearby church hall which was available on week days. Chock-a-block with furniture, including three pianos, it needed a firm of removers to stack it all in a smaller room. There were enough chairs, and I provided strengthened paper-hanging tables. The heating arrangements were archaic. Cast-iron gas fires suspended from the ceiling were turned on and off by using a long pole to pull on a chain. I was terrified of tugging too hard at some that had become stiff after use, in case I pulled them down and blew the place up! The hall was too large for blackboard and chalk so I changed to an overhead projector and screen. The classes, of up to thirty enthusiastic students, went well. However, with no safe storage there, the books and charts had to be carted home to Bosham each evening; and with the hall in use each Sunday, the chairs had to be stacked and the tables dismantled after class on Friday nights. It seemed an impractical way to live.

In 1975 I was left a small legacy with which I had built an extension to my house in Bosham, and obtained planning permission to hold evening classes at Windrift. There was space for about twelve cars in the drive. The others used the village car park and approached via the long dark country footpath. To guide them down the path to my house on the first evening I rigged a pair of leading lights, nautical style, in my garden. The new hall measured twenty-six by fifteen feet, which was perfectly adequate. I raised the charges each year, hoping to restrict the numbers; with so many RYA assessment papers to correct for each student in my own time after classes, work was long and hard.

Unless students asked, I thought it important that individual navigational problems were not discussed openly in class for fear of discouragement. People learn at different speeds, and slow ones often do better than those who are quicker but do not retain. Patient and tenacious home study is so important. When correcting the assessment papers I sometimes redrew the faulty chartwork or rewrote the answers. I would then go through the papers in class and each student could follow where they had gone wrong from my written corrections on their own paper. This was an added burden for me, but the sea is potentially dangerous and has to be taken seriously.

In September each year enrolment took place for the thirty weeks of evening classes from September to April for RYA Beginners, Yachtmaster Offshore and Ocean shorebased courses.

Meanwhile, my private tuition was growing. This suited students who could not attend evening classes or those particularly from overseas who wanted concentrated courses. They bought the hours in advance and then came at times to suit themselves; increasingly this seemed to work. Professional yacht crews from all over the world started to come for tuition. Often they crewed large ocean going yachts, both sail and power, but could not become skippers until they had their ticket. For three or four weeks they would stay in Bosham for four hours daily tuition and spend the rest of their time on home study. The word soon spread and quite a few came over for the Yachtmaster Offshore course, returning later for the Yachtmaster Ocean. Generally they worked hard as their living depended on the outcome. One young man turned up on the doorstep and said, 'heard of you in America. When can I start?' Inquiries often came by telephone, sometimes from a vessel at sea. One inquiry from a crew member on a yacht in the South Atlantic revealed I had taught both his skipper and his mate. However, the work was taxing with large spells of overload during which I would teach one person during the morning, another in the afternoon and then go straight on to three hours of evening classes. After clearing up and preparing for the next morning's tuition I was often too tired to eat, and I still had to find time for the endless correcting of papers and chartwork.

In the summer of 1975 I ran my first five day RYA practical afloat course to Cherbourg and back. One student owned a 32 foot Contessa, and with four other class members who had passed the Yachtmaster Offshore theory, hired me to assess their practical.

To continue these RYA five day practical afloat courses I chartered yachts, often from owners who had little time to use them. At that time sea schools usually chartered vessels for the whole season, paying in advance. They offered weekly courses and hoped to get enough people to fill them, employing shore staff to deal with the inquiries, bookings, cleaning and revictualling of the yachts, allowing the instructors to step aboard at the start of each course and disembark at the end.

I ran my school singlehanded, mainly to avoid being left with paper work and logistics only. I wanted to go to sea and liked the variety of my work. Anyway, as I had no capital I only chartered a yacht when I had enough takers to fill it. I needed at least three students for each afloat course to cover the costs of charter, food, fuel and any marina we put into. The RYA allowed a maximum of five people plus one instructor per course. I could not manage the practical afloat courses week in and week out during the summer, as I had to have time in which to turn round. I was virtually on twenty-four hour duty on board and by the time the course ended I was pretty flaked out. Then I had to clean ship and leave it in good order for the owner, remove my gear and return home to answer my correspondence and get ready for the next job. There was a limit to what I could handle. I found I had to build in a day or two either side of sea work to allow for any bad weather or maintenance delays. I had no time to be ill! How I would love a yacht on permanent charter which I could set up as I thought best with all my gear on board for the season.

By 1978 the demand had reached the point where in winter I was usually working a thirteen hour day. I decided to discontinue the evening classes and concentrate on private tuition for the theory courses. Individual tuition would eliminate the slog of correcting papers in my 'spare' time. I would have fewer people but could charge more. Beginners' courses were thirty-six hours' tuition, with forty-eight hours for the Yachtmasters Offshore and Ocean, spread as the student wished, day or evening, and changed at short notice when required. Private teaching gave me the flexibility to go to sea between early September and April should the opportunity arise. No longer was I trapped six months ahead to unremitting theory work. In 1979 I sailed to Alderney three times in quick succession, once for fun in *Pintail*, once for work with students in a chartered Rival 32, and once for the RNXS in *Portisham*. My acquaintances there wondered what I would turn up in next.

14

At Sea with RNXS

In the summer of 1976 I spent two weeks in *Portisham*, the first week sailing to Alderney, Plymouth, round Land's End and up to Barry in the Bristol Channel where we were involved in NATO exercises. When they ended we had a longish passage to Binic, Baie de St Brieuc, Brittany before returning to Portsmouth. I was Mate for the first time since qualifying and during my watches I conned and navigated the ship. The lock at Binic was closed the evening of our arrival. The Skipper did not wish to anchor and went below to his cabin instructing me as Officer of the Watch to sail where I chose provided *Portisham*, without fail, was back in time for the first opening of the lock in the morning. I was delighted to be in sole charge of the bridge for the first time and we steamed quietly through the night on a navigational exercise I devised, taking care to avoid the tide ridden rocks off this coastline.

In 1977 RNXS ships took part in the Silver Jubilee Fleet Review at Spithead. We were on board *Portisham* from Thursday 23 to Wednesday 29 June taking various members of HM Forces and their families to see the Fleet. We rehearsed for the Day and acted as a patrol vessel for the week clearing the channels between the anchored ships where yachts, dinghies and motor vessels were all manoeuvring for a look. I was Officer of the Watch when one little dinghy without looking tacked under our bow. It was an emergency 'stop both engines' then, 'full astern both engines'. Smoke belched from the diesel exhausts as they roared astern, the twin propellers thrashing to take the way off the ship just in time.

While preparing for the RNXS five day skipper's course which was to take place in late July 1978, I sailed to Chatham for Navy Days as Mate. *Portisham* took the public on twenty-minute trips round the harbour with a running commentary on the history of Chatham Naval Base and the RNXS. The Skipper allowed me to take command under his watchful eye for some of these sorties. It gave me excellent shiphandling practice in and out of tight berths and in dodging spectator craft. I always enjoyed Navy Days and later skippered *Portisham* on many such occasions at Portsmouth.

When I passed the skipper's course and became qualified to command Royal Naval Auxiliary Service ships, the Ministry of Defence invited national and local press, radio and television to watch me take *Portisham* out for the first time as Skipper. It was a daunting prospect. On Wednesday 23 August I was to move *Portisham* from her berth at Royal Clarence Yard, Gosport and put her alongside Marlborough Pier on the Portsmouth side of the harbour. This meant a sternboard out of Royal Clarence Yard, turning and proceeding southwards almost to the harbour entrance before crossing to get a good lead in to the pier avoiding the tidal set into Camber Creek just before reaching the berth. It was a beautiful day with crowds at Vernon and Marlborough Pier, but I just concentrated on the job in hand and refused to be distracted until the last warp was on and *Portisham* safely secured alongside. 'Finished with wheel, finished with engines', I said. 'That was a good alongside,' remarked a rather disappointed member of the press!

104

At a conference after the TV and radio interviews on board, the press asked many serious questions except one reporter who wanted to know if I wore lipstick at sea. We returned on board for a trip up the harbour, as the TV and radio reporters wanted to record the spoken helm and engine orders. Cable was rigged all over the bridge and my view ahead was obstructed by people with cameras standing on top of the charthouse immediately in front of the bridge. The sunny day had brought out every kind of pleasure boat as well as the usual naval vessels and ferries. It would require all my concentration to manoeuvre and I felt restricted in my vision and movement, so as a precaution I said, 'if I ask you to clear the bridge, please clear it fast.' Off we went and the television crew and the photographers kept asking me to turn the ship as the sun was in the wrong position for their cameras. I was glad to get back to the berth.

As a result of the publicity I was invited to the Women of the Year lunch at the Savoy where more than six hundred women were gathered. Dame Naomi James gave a horrific account of her scaling the mast of her yacht *Crusader* in atrocious weather to effect repairs after her starboard lower shrouds had parted, midway between New Zealand and Cape Horn in the fiercesome southern ocean during her epic round the world voyage singlehanded.

As seatime for skippers had already been allocated for that year, I had to wait until the following season. Suddenly an RNXS skipper on *Portisham* dropped out and I stood in for a few days to exercise with the Royal Naval Reserve. This took us up and around Southampton water including the back of the oil refinery jetties where passage was not normally permitted. All the berthing and turning in restricted waters was useful experience in command before *Portisham*'s winter refit.

The small Littlehampton Unit shared seatime with the large

105

Southampton Unit, while the Isle of Wight, also small, shared with Portsmouth. After I became Skipper and Head of afloat training I suggested that we should combine with the Isle of Wight. We had skippers and mates and they had charge engineers. This would relieve Southampton and Portsmouth who each had more than enough resources of their own. The powers that be agreed and it worked out very well, the Isle of Wight coming over on the ferry to join ship at Royal Clarence Yard, Gosport.

There were RNXS training passages to France, Belgium and Holland. As a visiting warship we were entertained occasionally by the local dignitaries in France and by the Dutch Navy in Holland. Sailing to Binic again, as skipper this time, was an interesting exercise in ship handling. Not only was the lock narrow with little clearance either side of *Portisham*, but a marina had just been built in the basin and this now protruded into the fairway at the exit from the lock. *Portisham's* length meant turning while part of the ship was still in the lock to avoid the yachts. Much slow ahead here and slow astern there were needed to ease her out without touching either the lock sides or the yachts in the marina. As the mayor had invited the ship's company to a reception, we in turn asked them back on board for drinks. Most of the town turned up including the mayor and the chief of police. In Binic the fire brigade provide the water and after they had replenished our tanks, they too joined the party. Our return to Portsmouth was in thick fog most of the way with much shipping to negotiate crossing the Channel. Special sea duty (SSD) men closed up to fog routine. Each crew member is selected for SSD as shown on the watch and station bill. This is their main task during any exacting circumstances or emergencies which require the best crewman for each job.

On a visit to Scheveningen, the Dutch Navy made us very welcome, and again there was a jolly return party on *Porti-*

sham. The next morning the ship was jammed between the dock wall astern and a large fishing vessel immediately ahead offloading her catch. The few inches of clearance fore and aft made it impossible for us to extricate ourselves under power. Deciding to warp out the vessel, I asked for a bow line to be run as far along the stern quay as possible. It was six in the morning and the high chain link fences obstructing the quayside were still locked. Nothing daunted, the crew tackled the assault course with enthusiasm and reached a distant fixture to give the warp a good lead. A few turns on the windlass swung the bow out to free us. As we manoeuvred to leave, the harbour master threw on board a huge plastic bag of fresh fish. 'For your lunch,' he shouted.

We were sailing to Ostend at night in another RNXS ship, *Loyal Mediator*, a trawler type vessel, 75 feet overall. Just discernible in the dark, a fast motor boat showing no lights was keeping station with us. To find out what was going on I stopped engines and immediately a French Customs vessel ranged alongside and we were boarded by an officer and a seaman with a walkie-talkie. The officer was extremely polite but persistent, asked endless questions about our length, tonnage and engines, where the ship was built, who we were, where from and whither bound, which I struggled to answer in French. They showed no signs of budging, so I asked the communicator to inform Dover coastguard on the VHF that one of Her Majesty's ships had been boarded and detained by the French Customs. In mid-conversation the French seaman received a message over his walkie-talkie, and after a rapid report to his officer they made to leave the bridge rattled and embarrassed. I shook hands with them as they departed as rapidly as they had arrived. Apparently French Customs had wind of a fishing vessel smuggling and they suspected us even though we were in uniform.

On another occasion *Portisham* arrived at St Peter Port,

Guernsey, on a weekend visit. Early next morning the shipping forecast reported a low approaching at 45 knots and that the wind would increase to southwest force 9, before veering northwest later. I reckoned that if we left immediately we would just about make Wight before the following wind rose to full strength. Having checked with Guernsey airport's excellent met station who confirmed my assessment, we slipped hastily and proceeded towards the Alderney Race in dead calm with not a murmur from the crew who were losing a day in Guernsey. Once into the Channel, the wind progressively increased to southwest force 9 just before reaching the Isle of Wight. I had laid the course so that we were stern to the wind, but as the steep following seas overtook us it was heavy work for the helmsman to prevent the stern slewing. In the approach channel to Portsmouth harbour the sea was so violent that we had to use the engine controls to assist the helmsman to keep a straight course.

On passage in *Portisham* from Ouistreham to Dartmouth a crew member was taken ill. Three hours after he had gone below I was informed that he had been in great pain but had not liked to report it. I went below to find him plainly in agony, but we were only trained in first aid. The coastguard was called up to enable me to consult a doctor, and I arranged a diversion to Weymouth some two hours' steaming distance, where an ambulance would meet us. At 0200 hours the waiting ambulance rushed the crewman to hospital where a kidney stone was diagnosed. He was out within a few days.

The interservices yacht *Hornet* lay alongside *Portisham* at Alderney one day. Having deliberately kept the boat light for their race, their tanks were empty and they asked us for water. As they had no hose and ours were too big we pumped up our header tank and let it overflow into their buckets. Around midnight two of *Portisham*'s crew on rope watch saw a yachtsman fall off the high quay, luckily missing the ship and various protruding obstacles. He was drunk but extremely cheerful as they fished him out and gave him dry clothes. He was determined to use his small dinghy to row out to his yacht in the strong wind and rough sea. In his condition I judged he would never make it. As we were departing shortly I asked the local police if they would find him a berth ashore.

In 1982 I received the RNXS long service medal and two years later to my surprise was made Head of the Little-hampton Unit. This promotion meant the sort of paperwork I had been dodging most of my life. I tried to streamline the administration and concentrate on seagoing and instruction. When Chatham naval base closed, Littlehampton's shoreb-ased side was disbanded, and another change joined the Shore-ham Unit to us as well as the Isle of Wight.

Operation Brave Defender, the first major joint services exercise in the United Kingdom since the Second World War, was held in September 1985. I was *Portisham*'s delivery skip-per on passage from Portsmouth to Ipswich to enable the RNXS east coast units to take part in the exercise. We had a crew of ten for this voyage instead of the usual nineteen when training. Gales delayed us for twelve hours and we finally slipped from Royal Clarence Yard at 0900 hours and found southwesterly following winds. The shallow depression was moving rapidly east away from us. From North Foreland on passage across the Thames Estuary, we were headed by the winds now north northwest. The shipping forecast reported that the low had deepened unexpectedly and had turned back. The wind increased to gale force 8. Rough seas pounded over the high open bridge as *Portisham* fell into every hole. The AGMC compass and repeaters were non-operational, the mag-netic steering compass was difficult to read in the dark wet weather, and the helmsman found it heavy going. At mid-night, 10 miles off the Felixstowe approach channel, I went to slow down to give way to another vessel only to find that the starboard engine control was jammed. There was nothing for it but to close down the engine. We navigated the winding River Orwell to Ipswich in pitch blackness on one engine and secured alongside at 0200 hours. The Ministry of Defence had arranged for a woman reporter and a male photographer to ship aboard for this passage from Portsmouth. They were most interested in both the voyage and the Service, in spite of feeling seasick, and wrote an informative and complimentary article in the *East Anglian Daily Times*.

The 23 metre Loyal class fleet tenders had long been replacing the elderly inshore minesweepers. With a single screw, so less manoeuvrable and slower, but with good sea keeping qualities, they had powered steering and windlass and a closed in bridge. Although more comfortable we still preferred the inshore minesweepers, which we considered to be proper ships. Now a completely new class of smaller, lighter boats called P2000 were arriving. They were 20 metre, 20 knot patrol boats with twin engines, closed-in wheelhouse and open upper bridge. Highly manoeuvrable with sophisticated equipment, these vessels were more suited to our new Defence of Ports and Anchorages (DEFPA) role.

I was in the RNXS for nineteen years, most of them with the friendly and cheerful unit at Littlehampton, where I had the good fortune to be a Skipper for eleven years and Head of Unit for five. In 1989 my favourite *Portisham* and I reached retiring age.

15

Flying Light

For years John had been planning to have an ocean going yacht built to his design or to fit out a hull himself. But one-offs were time consuming and costly, and since he was hard pressed running his own engineering firm, spare time was short. In the January 1982 Boat Show at Earl's Court we saw a Beneteau First 42 foot fin keel sloop designed by German Frers. The yacht was simple and, without excessive freeboard, had sufficient head room for John to walk upright through the accommodation, which he liked. Later we went to Hamble for a trial sail in her. John refused to countenance a vessel lying on her mooring most of the time, but would order one if I agreed to charter her for my sea school courses. It was a wonderful offer which I accepted with alacrity. In that case, he said, I had better get on with it and fit her out, which I did. As we seemed to agree on most things, I went ahead and ordered what was needed while *Flying Light* was still on the production line. She arrived in May and as we got to know her, we discovered the good points of a clever design which was sea kindly and forgiving. Notwithstanding her fin keel and spade rudder, she hove to sweetly and would beat to windward efficiently under any sail including foresail only.

As I had no help it seemed sensible, although expensive, to keep *Flying Light* at a marina. Even if we could have found a deep water mooring in Bosham channel it would have been a very long way from the quay, and I would have needed a motor boat to take out students and gear. The bar at Chichester harbour entrance could be crossed only at certain states of the tide and was no place to return to in strong onshore weather with its tidal streams and shallow bottom causing a steep turbulent sea. We would have had to divert to Portsmouth harbour with subsequent problems of transport. For the same reasons the Chichester harbour marinas were also ruled out, so we settled for Camper and Nicholson's marina at Gosport, which was efficient and friendly and only forty minutes from Bosham by car. I was used to that journey as *Portisham* was berthed at Royal Clarence Yard just north of Camper's. I brought the stores for the course from home by car, heaved them aboard, stowed, stayed the night and greeted the students next morning.

Flying Light (or *Flight* for short) had a 50hp Perkins diesel engine, eight berths including two cabins with double berths, a galley, two heads and a large saloon with two pilot and two settee berths and a table. The full-sized chart table had stowage for Admiralty charts. A navel pipe was added to lead the 60 metres of ⅜ inch anchor chain below to the cable locker, and the 45lb anchor was stowed over the bow ready for instant use. At that time her main was slab reefed and her foresail roller furled. John rigged her as a cutter with a detachable inner forestay on which to set staysails.

My RYA five day afloat courses consisted of ship acquaint for the students on day one, followed by handling practice on all points of sailing, man overboard drill, reefing and gybing. Passage making next day was either westwards or to Cherbourg or Alderney, weather permitting, a student acting as skipper having prepared a passage plan. The course included deck work, handling under sail and power, rope work, night passages, anchoring in a chosen position, weather forecasts, lights, buoys and rules of the road and keeping the estimated position going while living at sea. Each crew member acted as skipper in turn and the weather threw in a few surprises like strong winds or poor visibility.

An hour after slipping the marina berth on one of these courses a crew member asked if there was usually so much water below. I hurtled down the companionway to discover it was above the cabin sole. A taste of the water established that it was fresh, so at least we were not sinking. A damp but systematic search located the leak at the junction of the filler pipe with the flexible water bags. We tightened the joint, pumped the ship dry and had a lovely sail to Cherbourg and Alderney. Later these water bags were replaced with two fifty gallon stainless steel tanks. Coming home, *Flying Light* took the force 7 northeasterly head wind in her stride. Coming alongside the home berth at about one o'clock in the morning a hefty crew member leapt ashore with the stern rope and promptly disappeared into the water under the stern of a moored yacht. I was at the wheel and before I had time to react, the marina berthing master with impeccable timing rounded the corner on one of his security checks and hauled him out complete with oilskins, boots, lifejacket and harness. Meanwhile I was asking another crew member to 'take a turn, take a turn,' meaning take one turn of the mooring rope round the pontoon cleat to hold the yacht alongside in the strong offshore wind. I got no response whatever. Poor girl, far from taking a turn, she too had slipped on the seaweed strewn pontoon and was hanging on to the yacht's guard rail for dear life with her feet in the water trying to avoid a ducking.

We had some quick changing weather on one seven day course. After a pleasant sail to Cherbourg we left the next day for Alderney. Soon after leaving the marina and while still in the Rade de Cherbourg, the enormous outer harbour, fog came down and we were hard pressed to find our way back to our berth. When it cleared we set off in light airs for Alderney and in the dim light of evening picked up a mooring which we mistook for a visitor's buoy. That night without warning, the wind increased to 35 knots northeasterly, to which direction the harbour was completely open. I was in the cockpit checking when the mooring parted. The rocky shoreline was close under our stern. I started the engine immediately and we motored to the quay, securing outside some fishing vessels and spent the night fending off with our feet in the strong surge running through the harbour. In the morning, exhausted, we moved to the proper visitor's mooring while the gale raged on.

Two of the crew had departed for home, the third would soon run out of time as well, and I would have to singlehand back if the wind did not abate. But after a gale tossed night the early morning was calm and the Alderney lighthouse fog horn started to sound. We tacked most of the way back in quite strong winds, having started out with none at all. By the time we were approaching Sandown Bay and Bembridge Ledge buoy, Isle of Wight, it was calm and there was thick fog again.

In June 1985 I sailed *Flying Light* to St Katherine's Dock, London with Geraldine and two of our friends, John and Robin Bishop. We started up channel from Gosport on a roller-coaster ride with a following wind gusting force 7. The crew suggested entering Brighton marina for the night to wait for the wind to moderate. I was not keen as the entrance was reputed to be tricky in rough onshore weather causing a dangerous sea to build up between the piers. Its reputation proved well founded, and it took all my experience to get in safely. The next day was settled and we sailed past Beachy Head and Dungeness and northwards through the Gull

Stream, turning west before Tongue Sand Tower against an unremitting head sea to enter the fast flowing Thames, through the new flood control barrier to lock in at St Katherine's Dock after 220 miles. What struck me was the sad lack of shipping and the empty docks; the mighty Thames beaten flat.

I had been getting restless, restricted as I was to short passages for my work. The Yachtmaster Ocean 600 miles qualifying course I offered found little response. John had mentioned his idea of re-rigging *Flying Light* to make short-handed work less arduous. I wanted to enter for the next Observer singlehanded transatlantic race starting on 5 June 1988 from Plymouth to Newport, Rhode Island, under new sponsorship from Carlsberg; but it was only a dream, as I would need a boat. John offered to lend me *Flying Light* and in his usual generous offhand way said it would encourage him to make the modifications he wanted. For this venture he said that he would be the ground crew and I would be the pilot!

16

Gibraltar and Back

In July 1986 I applied to the Royal Western Yacht Club of England at Plymouth to enter the 1988 Carlsberg single-handed transatlantic race, giving my sea experience as requested and paying my deposit. I was accepted. Entry qualifications for the Race after any major modifications to the yacht required both a cruise of 1000 miles and a minimum of 500 miles singlehanded without anchoring or putting into port.

Out to Gibraltar

I had set my heart on sailing non-stop to Gibraltar, two handed outward bound and singlehanded back. The first half of the 1,200 miles homeward passage would be against the prevailing winds and currents and so nearer to conditions I might expect when tackling the North Atlantic. An insurance company agreed to cover me for the singlehanded work, both for the return from Gibraltar and for the transatlantic race. Without this cover I felt unable to borrow the vessel.

Flying Light's design, a First 42, had been developed from an International Offshore Racing yacht called *Gitana*, a two ton cup winner. *Flight* had a shallow dinghy-like hull, fin keel and spade rudder, beamy but with fine ends. Her displacement was only eight tons when empty and she needed a full crew for performance. But for long distance and singlehanded work she became completely manageable when loaded with ocean going equipment; then she was docile, stable and stiff, with good close winded performance. She was 42 feet overall (12.8 metres), 36 feet on the waterline, with a 13 foot beam. *Flight* was the 5 feet 8 inches draught version with a longer fin keel than the deep draught option. She was re-rigged as a cutter. To simplify and modify *Flying Light* John ordered a Hood stowaway mast stepped through deck, unlike the original mast stepped on deck. He also ordered Hood roller-furling foresails, a genoa and a staysail, which meant that all working sails could be set, reefed and furled without leaving the cockpit. There were to be four extra sails, a trysail, storm foresail, light weather genoa and a cruising chute, all requiring deck working.

We already had virtually unused an Autohelm 5000 autopilot which John decided to update to the more sophisticated 6000 model with a microprocessor. This provided automatic sensitivity feedback enabling it to learn from its own performance and make sensitive corrections to suit the prevailing sea state. A Firdell radar reflector was secured to the 52 foot mast as high up as possible. At sea in RNXS ships I had noticed that an intermittent blip on the radar screen, sometimes with a long interval between the blips, often turned out to be a yacht masked as it disappeared into the troughs. The danger was it could easily be dismissed as interference or clutter. John did not want the reflector on the mainmast in case of halyard snarl-up, but compromised by setting a guard round it.

To warn of approaching traffic when off watch, a radar was

fitted with an automatic alarm system. Two adjustable guard rings were set to suitable ranges so that vessels entering the guard zone between the two rings activated an alarm bleeper. John refused point blank this time to secure the radar scanner to the mast and decided on a pole aft to rise fifteen feet above the deck. This was a back door way in to installing a mizzenmast, which he particularly favoured. He had been dying to turn *Flight* into a double headed yawl like *Pintail*. I preferred a cutter rig with a taller mast although I agreed that a mizzen broke up the sail plan and made it more manageable when cruising shorthanded. In difficult weather the main could be handed and the vessel sailed on foresail and mizzen alone. However, with a stowaway mast there would be no need to struggle on deck to reef the mainsail in heavy weather. I hated the idea of a mizzenmast spoiling the yacht's lines, but I should have known better; John's design looked very good indeed. No sail was carried on the mizzenmast but halyards were rigged so that it could serve as a jury mast if the mainmast was lost. A large deck light fixed to the mizzenmast floodlit the cockpit.

The power consumption of the radar and other instruments required a small generator to charge the batteries and avoid the need to run the main engine on light load, which is not good for diesels. To brief the shipyard, John produced many of the working drawings for re-siting the winches and fairleads to accommodate the new sail plan, and electrical diagrams for the generator as well as the radar mast aft. Other modifications included a lookout dome in place of the saloon hatch and perspex washboards to enable a lookout to be kept and the rig checked when closed up in storm force conditions. Everything heavy on board was secured to withstand a 360° roll in case of knockdown. An obligatory watertight forward bulkhead was constructed and emergency deadlights made for all hatches and ports.

The shipyard work was in the care of George Truckell, the capable manager of the Ancasta Marine Services yard at Cowes. Rigging was by Spencers of Cowes, electrical work by Martec, and Malcolm Lane of Regis dealt ably with all the electronic instrumentation. Technical conferences were held frequently in Cowes with George and his team, and the countless problems which arose in the modification of the yacht were overcome one by one.

Navigation instruments comprised a compass, a Brookes and Gatehouse echo sounder, an inboard patent log and a spare Stowe towed log, a sextant, a deck watch and stop watch, and a Brookes and Gatehouse Homer 5, long range receiver for weather forecasts with a Heron direction finding (DF) attachment. Although not a fan of DF, I thought it would be useful to confirm my estimated position in poor visibility when approaching the shore. Also fitted was a VHF radio telephone. A great many Admiralty charts, large and small scale, were bought together with Admiralty tide tables and tidal stream atlases, Admiralty lists of lights, lists of radio signals and sailing directions, precomputed sight reduction tables Naval Publication 401, the nautical almanac, plotting sheets for astronomical sights and routeing charts of the North Atlantic for July and August showing prevailing winds and currents in the areas. Because of the high costs involved, the shipyard work was planned in two phases, before and after the qualifying Gibraltar voyage. However, for various good reasons, parts of phase two were added to phase one, the structural alterations, and we were three weeks late. Unfortunately this left no time for trials.

On 24 July 1987 we slipped Cowes marina with log reading zero. Instead of sailing straight for Ushant, we decided that a shakedown track along the English shore would be prudent to try out all the new equipment. In fact we had some minor problems which we could resolve ourselves given sheltered water, so we anchored just inside the Helford River to sort things out.

On 28 July, with log reading 165.97, we weighed anchor and set sail for Gibraltar. I wanted to pass 60 miles off Ushant to clear the traffic separation scheme which extended some 35 miles offshore and to get a reasonable offing in case of bad weather. With the prevailing southwesterly winds and current both setting into the Bay of Biscay, we needed enough sea room should severe conditions force us to heave to or lie a hull (under bare poles). It so happened there was a high pressure system, the clockwise circulation giving following winds mainly from the north and northwest with moderate sea conditions, and we covered some 360 nautical miles in two and a half days. Three days out of Helford in the waters off Cape Finisterre the wind increased to northeast force 7 and then gale force 8 during the night, the seas steep and rough. *Flying Light* ran before the wind on autopilot under reefed main and foresails and then under staysail only, the vessel's speed controlled by furling and unfurling the staysail from the companionway. She was fast and buoyant and her stern lifted unerringly to the enormous following seas. The motion was so comfortable below it was difficult to realise what the weather was like outside. Batteries were monitored and the generator started when they needed charging, and the running hours logged for fuel consumption.

By noon next day, 1 August, the wind had abated and the sun shone, a lovely day, but the swell was heavy. By night the sea had moderated and we sailed by moonlight. We could see the dolphins gambolling round the log line in the light of the masthead tricolour so we handed the log in case they decided to have the rotator for supper. Winds then became variable in strength and direction until we reached the Straits of Gibraltar at night with a gusty westerly force 5–6. Steered by the amazing Autohelm 6000, we kept as near as possible to the edge of the traffic separation scheme to make full use of the east going current. At no time since leaving home waters had we hand steered. Early on 6 August we secured alongside Marina Bay marina after clearance at Waterport Reporting Point, nine days out of Helford River, with log reading 1199.03.

I was eager to return as soon as possible, and John, who had to fly back to London, booked in on Sunday's only plane. All this meant a quick turn round of three days. The new generator had to be serviced, the yacht refuelled and revictualled and clothes washed.

John discovered the forward head's basin let the water out with the seacock closed, thereby undermining the watertight integrity of the vessel. We spent most of one day trying to persuade the only yacht yard to lift *Flying Light* out of the water for an engineer to check the seacock. They were up to their eyes in work; it was Friday when at closing time most of the workforce would return to Spain for their weekend. Late that afternoon they good-naturedly squeezed us in to their schedule, only to discover that at some time a screw had been dropped down the basin pipe and had lodged in the gate valve, thus preventing it from closing. All that effort and expense was for one small screw.

The fresh food had lasted quite well on our outward voyages. I had also stowed aboard thirty large packets of pure orange juice and thirty large bottles of soda water in case of water tank failure of some kind, or great delay. *Flight* had two 50 gallon stainless steel tanks, and we carried a spare five gallon plastic can of water. I was somewhat wary of buying cooked meats and pies in Gibraltar for the return voyage because of the hot weather. I am not usually fussy but did not want to go down with stomach trouble when on my own. I carried a comprehensive medicine chest, but luckily had no health problems on any of the voyages.

Home from Gibraltar

Soon after first light on 9 August, I slipped Marina Bay on the start of my singlehanded non-stop voyage to Portsmouth. I was so looking forward to it. Having seen his lovely yacht sailing away, poor John was left to kick his heels for twelve hours before catching his flight back.

The current in the middle of the Straits flows eastwards as evaporation lowers the water level of the Mediterranean, allowing the Atlantic to flow in. This evaporation results in the surface water becoming saline and dense; it sinks, causing a subsurface flow of bottom water westwards back into the Atlantic. However, inshore tidal streams, similar to our own waters, change direction every so many hours. Once clear of Gibraltar Bay I wanted to catch the inshore southwest going stream which served three hours after local high water.

On both voyages, outward and inward bound, I kept a plot on largish scale Admiralty charts. The estimated position including true course steered, leeway if any, log distance and currents or tidal streams were entered in the log book with wind direction and strength and barometric pressure. The estimated position was checked with astro sights when the visibility was clear. I also kept the plot going for each voyage on a small scale chart 4103, English Channel to Gibraltar and the Azores, which showed the track. These charts of the outward and inward voyages were signed by yard and marina managers at the start and finish of each voyage as verification for the Royal Western Yacht Club. I found it an awful fag to keep the two plots going simultaneously.

Once out of the Straits, I was caught up in the opposing flow of traffic sweeping round Cape St. Vincent to Cape Trafalgar and struggled unsuccessfully to get well offshore. It meant keeping a vigilant lookout both visual and on radar as some ships passed very close indeed on both sides of me. Early next evening the barometer fell and the wind increased to northwest force 6. In lumpy seas I reefed the main, furled the genoa and left only the staysail set. As the wind increased to force 7 (33 knots) I was engulfed in a thunderstorm. The lightning was spectacular, illuminating the darkness as the rain came down like stair rods. The radar alarm shrieked and I could see large furry shapes tracking across the screen like a horror film. There were no ships about, the thunder clouds had activated the alarm. I put the perspex washboards in place and closed the air vents to keep out the rain and the seas crashing down on deck. Wedged in at the chart table as the vessel heeled, I could see enormous seas rushing past the saloon ports on the lee side. I decided to have a ten minute nap as there had been no chance to sleep since I started. When I awoke we were making little progress against a heavy head sea. To keep way on in the shelter of the deep troughs I needed to pluck up courage and set more sail. This I did, and *Flight* responded immediately by surging forward and crashing her way noisily through the crests. Now I was engaged in finding a compromise between limiting the stress on the vessel and making headway. The result of the night's storm was a fine coating of yellow sand, presumably from the Sahara, over the deck and sails.

Three days out from Gibraltar with light and variable winds I was constantly trimming the sails in an effort to get *Flying Light* moving. To get further offshore I should set the new cruising chute which we had raised for the first time on the outward passage. It was a large volatile sail which I had not practised hoisting on my own. The winds were variable in direction and I did not want to end up with the sail snarled up in the rig aloft. Reluctantly I decided against it.

Sleep was something I worried about when sailing singlehanded. I had been trained to keep a proper lookout at sea as required by the International Regulations for the Prevention of Collision at Sea. In good visibility I had something like twenty minutes' closing time between *Flying Light* and the fastest ship when first seen over the horizon. I had two alarm pingers with different tones which I set at twenty minutes having first scanned an empty horizon, but I was usually awake in half that time. My last line of defence was the radar guard zone alarm which would sound if a ship approached within six miles. I lay down in the after cabin, which was nearest to the companionway, fully clothed including shoes and safety harness. When I woke I could shoot straight out of the berth and be on deck instantly. Later I increased the alarm time to one hour where there appeared to be no traffic, but seldom slept for more than thirty minutes.

Navigation kept me busy as well as sail trimming in light variable winds. In strong weather I went out to the cockpit at intervals day or night to check that all was well and to reef sails and trim sheets when needed. I did not feel tired and the days passed quickly. However, I knew that in the long term I needed more sleep and would have to place greater reliance on my multi-alarm system. On two occasions I overslept for about three hours with no recollection of having done so; I just noticed the clock hands had moved on. Washing was the catlick and a promise sort with little water, and changes of clothes had to wait for calmer weather.

Four days out, in the early evening, the autopilot ceased to function. It would be exhausting to continue for some 800 or 900 miles without self-steering. In mid-Atlantic I would have no choice, but here I was within reach of land. I checked on the chart for the nearest large port to put into for repairs. This was Libson. The distance was some 40 miles to the entrance of the River Tagus and another 12 miles up river to Belem Basin which the pilot book recommended. I handed the sails and swilled around in the ocean calm while making a detailed passage plan to enter the river just before dawn on a flood tide. I laid off tracks and a clearing bearing on the powerful Cascais light. The bearing was within the safe white sector of the light, which I hoped to pick up when closer in. This would clear me to seaward of the entrance buoy which, I later discovered, had been removed, and position me on the leading lights and marks up river. Luckily I had included a large scale chart of the entrance to the Tagus in case of difficulties. I had something to eat and a ten minute nap as I was short of sleep as usual and would be up all night steering. Without wind it would have to be a motoring job.

After a night at the wheel I picked up Cascais light. Altering course as necessary on the bearing to keep on track, I arrived at the entrance as dawn broke, when down came the fog. It was difficult finding my way up the fast flowing river with its many drying heights on the sharp bend to starboard. I could not leave the wheel for more than a minute to navigate as *Flight* quickly went off course. I rigged the mooring ropes and fenders off Belem Dock, the visibility having cleared near the town. I found it difficult to berth *Flying Light* single-handed with no one ashore to take the lines. She is fairly high and beamy and tapers sharply at the ends, so it is necessary to bring her alongside exactly parallel to the berth before disembarking amidships. It was not easy for me to leave the wheel, get to midships with the bow and stern warps and leap ashore before the vessel drifted out of position. Eventually after much gesticulating and calling in English and in French, which no one understood, I got some help and secured alongside the only space available – the oil pontoon – at 0930 hours Friday 14 August. I had logged 420 miles from Gibraltar, just 80 miles short of the qualifying distance. Now I would have to restart from Libson.

I could speak no Portuguese, and it was their equivalent of

a bank holiday so most people were away. I spent the best part of two days on the telephone at Lisbon Naval Club trying to get help to resolve the autopilot defect. Autohelm had no agent in Lisbon. If replacements were to be flown from England I had to find someone who could fit them. I gloomily mentioned this to a young Frenchman moored opposite on a 60 foot yacht he had sailed singlehanded from France. 'I will look,' he said, leaping enthusiastically on board. Having found nothing wrong with the electronics he heaved out a mass of heavy spare gear, unbolted the deck boards in the after locker or lazarette and literally stood on his head to see what was amiss below. He discovered that the fitting on the end of the autopilot motor arm had sheered the machine screws attaching it to the steering quadrant: a straightforward job. When the shops opened on Monday he bought the screws and mended it. 'It will last one gale, maybe two,' he announced. In fact it lasted through three gales and was still working when I reached home. He introduced me to an English widow who had lived in Lisbon for many years. She took me off in a taxi to the supermarket two or three miles away to victual. It was a great kindness from two complete strangers.

There seemed no point in trials: either it would work or it would not. Visibility was clear on Tuesday 18 August as I sailed down river on the stern transit clearing the drying heights off Fort Bugio. Barely had I emerged from the river entrance when the wind increased to north northwest force 7–8 with a rough sea. Close hauled with reefed main and staysail, *Flight* was making 6 knots out to longitude 11°W, a good offing clear of the traffic lanes.

Next day the wind fell light and I went about on to port tack which took me in to longitude 10°W; then as the wind backed I was able to lay a northerly course some 60 miles off the Iberian coast. It was a lovely sail with blue skies, but the seas were still quite rough with a high swell. Four days out

127

of Lisbon the winds fell light, the sea like jelly. In the distance I could see two large dolphins standing off while five fatso cuddly babies put on a water ballet for me by the stern. I wanted to dive in and join them and could have stayed out there forever.

Five days out, just past Finisterre, the southwesterly wind strengthened to force 6 with driving rain. It was a nice run but not for long as the wind soon veered to north northwest gale force to head us again. I had to bear away 30° for a fast container ship coming at us head on. The seas were tremendous, as high as houses, but *Flying Light* did not seem to mind as she climbed steadily over them, so I decided I would not mind either. The tops of the seas crashed down on the deck.

Suddenly the heavy gas cooker went askew on its gimbals. The support screws had worked loose and were inaccessible. If it broke free immense damage would be done and the gas line would fracture, so I lashed the whole thing to the fixed guard rail. Without gimbals, I had to hold the pans while cooking; as that was too time consuming, I ate the food cold. When the generator was running I could use the electric kettle on the 240 volts supply, but I decided that an electric saucepan would be a better back up in future.

It had been difficult to lay the northerly track and I had been driven unwillingly into the flow of shipping between Ushant and Finisterre. There was now 40 knots of wind blowing from the north and a heavy swell when the shipping forecast announced that a cold front was blocked over the British Isles, sending all the depressions to Biscay; quite unnecessary! The wind veered to north northeast and for more than twenty-four hours persisted at gale force 8.

Seven days out the wind abated to force 5 and we made better progress with all sails set in sunshine but with a big swell still running. 'Low Rockall 1003 expected Plymouth by

1300 hours tomorrow', said the forecast; this was a shallow low near enough to affect me. That evening the wind increased to 30 knots; close hauled under reefed main and staysail it became a roller-coaster ride. Having dropped most of the shipping I had a short sleep; but I was now approaching the tidal streams off Ushant, at springs, setting east and west alternately. With 40 knots of wind the port tack edged me towards the traffic separation scheme, while the less favourable starboard set me in the direction of America. The yacht was making leeway and it was a struggle to make headway in the rough seas. The low promised to fill but was having death throes.

Ten days out of Lisbon, I cleared Ushant and the morning dawned bright and cheerful with light to moderate winds. Instead of sailing obliquely up channel I decided to close the English coast to be within range of coast radio stations for a VHF link call to the owner informing him his yacht was still afloat. I gave up trying to sleep during the last night, a Saturday, since there were too many yachts and ships between Portland Bill and the Solent, and cleaned ship instead. Landfall was made at Bridge buoy, off the Needles at dawn in poor visibility which turned into thick fog off Yarmouth Roads. John had advised me on VHF to get past Cowes before the start of the power boat race.

The fog lifted and I secured alongside Camper and Nicholson's marina, Gosport at 1000 hours on Sunday 30 August. The log read 2,776 miles including nearly 400 miles more than the outward voyage because of so much tacking and the diversion to Lisbon. I really liked it out there on my own and was looking forward to the transatlantic race, although I realised that with the contrary winds it would be tough, with ice and fog on the Newfoundland Banks as an added hazard.

Before leaving on the Gibraltar qualifying voyage I had cancelled my school advertisements in the yachting press.

Although I taught navigation theory up to my departure time, *Flying Light*, undergoing modifications, was not available for the practical sea work. My qualifying passages were accepted by the Royal Western Yacht Club and I paid the rest of the entry fee. Geraldine thought I would survive but was unsure whether she would! Hugh was concerned that without sufficient sleep I might start to hallucinate. Both seemed to have faith in my abilities.

17

Singlehanded Transatlantic

Second phase modifications to *Flying Light* started in January 1988. John decided to add some electronic navigation instruments for use in poor visibility when it would be impossible to get astro sights. When sailing singlehanded it is difficult to know exactly what course has been steered if the autopilot has followed the wind. Without this vital information for estimated position no accurate plot could be maintained. Electronics are marvellous but the basics are needed in case of failure. My reaction was to take a second sextant which, in the event, Bosham Sailing Club generously gave me.

Because, unlike previous races, Carlsberg were not providing the Argos satellite tracking system which monitored each vessel's position, yachts in Classes I, II and III only (I was in Class III) were obliged to install a high frequency single side-band radiotelephone to report their position daily to Portishead Radio, with a time penalty for failure to do so. An Icom 150 watt radiotelephone with a range of several thousand miles was installed in *Flight* at great expense. Other modifications included an auxiliary fuel tank to provide a total of eighty-five gallons for the diesel driven generator. Fresh water transfer pumps were installed between the tanks under the forward bunks, obligatory under Royal Western Yacht Club race rules which treated fresh water as movable ballast. Backup systems were added: an electric jug for cooking when the generator was running; a gimballed mini camping *gaz* stove which would take a kettle. Extra high fiddles were fitted and nets were fixed across the openings to the pilot berths in the saloon to provide further stowage. The yacht was equipped with a comprehensive set of tools including bolt croppers and a multitude of spares. A collision umbrella was carried for plugging a hole in the hull.

The self-inflatable liferaft had to contain a VHF Jotron emergency position indicating radio beacon (EPIRB) which transmitted automatically on 121.5mHz, the aircraft frequency, when the raft inflated. Mounted on the pushpit was a large Jotron emergency location transmitter operating on 406mHz which would detach itself if the vessel foundered and transmit a coded signal identifying the yacht's name and position via satellite to a shore station.

I carried Admiralty charts of the English and American coasts, North Atlantic charts, great circle Gnomonic charts, routeing charts for June, July and August which showed the prevailing winds and currents and areas where fog, ice and storms were most likely to occur along the route. I also carried admiralty lists of lights and radio signals, tide tables and tidal steam atlases and charts and publications in case breakdowns forced me to divert to ports off my track. These included coasts of Ireland, Brittany, the Azores, Newfoundland, Halifax and the Gulf of St Lawrence.

Shipyard work was again in the safe hands of George Truckell and his team at Ancasta yard, Cowes, with Spencers, Martec and Regis teams in support. John was responsible for the design work. Commander Sir David Mackworth generously offered John his expert advice in recalculating all the loads on *Flying Light*'s rigging. He decided that in the event of knockdown the margin on the lower shrouds was insufficient and advised that these shrouds should be doubled up to increase the safety factor. David's time, effort and professional expertise concluded with his scaling the mast in Plymouth for a final check immediately before the start.

Early on Saturday morning, 21 May, we sailed from Camper and Nicholson's marina at Gosport to Cowes for some last minute work, and at 1900 hours slipped for Plymouth, two weeks before the race. Competitors had to be in Plymouth by Saturday 28 May, eight days before the race started, but I wanted John to sail to Plymouth with me to use the voyage as a shakedown, and he could only manage a weekend. The southeasterly wind soon increased and backed to easterly 5–6 and then to gale force 8. After confused seas and a very rough, cold ride we secured alongside Queen Anne's Battery marina on Sunday evening, having averaged 6 knots under deeply reefed sails.

As the marina filled up, yachts had to be positioned so as to accommodate us all in this small space. Although 130 yachts were entered, only ninety-five actually started, including five women. A week before the start, John, Hugh, Geraldine and her friend Brian Dawson arrived to help prepare the boat. John worked flat out but needed professional help, so Brian Wyatt, an engineer from the Ancasta yard, and Malcolm Lane of Regis Electronics came to Plymouth and spent long hours struggling with various problems. Friends came down to cheer me on, and Carlsberg, the Royal Western Yacht Club and the Royal Naval Sailing Association (RNSA) all gave tremendous support. The atmosphere was friendly and frenetic. The camaraderie of international competition reminded me of my swimming and diving days.

Flying Light passed the Race inspection. As I had refused to have my propeller removed or my engine inhibited, *Flight's* gear lever was sealed in neutral by drilling a hole in the engagement button and inserting a locking wire. In an emergency I could cut this and use the engine for propulsion, in which case I would probably be disqualified.

The weather in Plymouth was atrocious; cold, wet and windy. I hoped it would improve before the start of the race as I had no racing skipper experience nor any wish to collide with other competitors jostling for position or with the crush of spectator boats. On the day before the race, preparation reached fever pitch. John was up all night finishing off last minute work, including stowing all the fresh food. Notwithstanding the noon start, the towing out process began at 0800 hours still to the sound of riveting and sawing as support crews tried frantically to complete their work. I asked John for a last minute change to the stowage position of the main hatchway washboards, and he was driving in the last of the fixing screws as the race motorboat came alongside to tow us out of the berth. A high pressure system had taken over, giving light winds. Friends and family transferred from *Flight* to a motor cruiser which we had hired as a support boat. As there was a lot of time before the starting gun we sailed up and down off Cawsand Bay in about 10 knots of wind before John too was taken off by the cruiser.

I was on my own bound for Newport Rhode Island. Race instructions were: leave Eddystone lighthouse and Nantucket Island to starboard.

Departure

My start was not exactly spectacular but not as fearsome as expected. The Royal Western had organised it well with the multihulls and monohulls separated at either end of the line and the spectator boats kept clear. My support boat followed me over the starting line as did friends' yachts and the BBC in a launch taking film. I was one of three competitors asked by them to take a video camera with me. The others were Tony Bullimore in the 60 foot trimaran *Apricot* and Pete Goss, a marine, in the 26 foot catamaran *Cornish Meadow*. A helicopter buzzed overhead taking photographs, having previously asked how to distinguish me from the air. The support boat followed me out a long way. There was much laughing and gesticulating as she tried to keep up with me, only turning back eventually at the limit of her fuel supply. The atmosphere was electric, with blue sea and sky, white sails, ninety-five yachts and all the spectator boats. Amid much waving of goodbyes and great excitement, a great adventure was starting. I felt completely calm, no doubts at all. I wanted so much to sail the North Atlantic. I had hankered after it for years.

It was a beautiful sunny afternoon and a fast sail with all three working sails set. Close hauled I made a course just west of south and decided to continue south southwest rather than tack close round Eddystone lighthouse and into the bay with the rest of the fleet. This was my last sight of the other yachts. The tidal stream was slackening before turning to the west, but as it would be strongly against me off the Lizard I had decided to give it a wide berth. Eventually the wind veered to west then northwest force 4 enabling me to lay a west southwesterly course to clear the Lizard by some 20 miles before turning to the west close hauled on starboard tack, making 7½–8 knots and clearing the traffic separation scheme south of the Scillies by four miles. In the early hours next day the wind died completely, the sea was like jelly and the sails limp, right in the approach to the separation scheme with all the big ships heading in and out of it.

I had trouble with the gas cooker that first day out. The support screws loosened again and would not hold, so I bolted and lashed it which meant it was no longer gimballed. The pans now had to be held on the stove, which was dangerous work in rough weather. This gave me no encouragement to cook anything other than coffee or eggs which heated up quickly. However, I could use the electric jug when the generator was running.

After twelve hours' unrelenting struggle to get *Flying Light* to move, the wind came up in the afternoon to force 4. There was much to do and I was very tired after only the odd ten minute catnap. Rain, drizzle and gloomy visibility persisted. I started on my great circle course across the Atlantic now that I was clear of the longitude of Scillies. Early next morning the wind had increased to force 6 and I was making 7½ knots but decided to furl the genoa leaving the full main and staysail. The lazy sheet snagged, preventing the proper stowing of the genoa, so I went forward to clear it.

Awaking from a short nap, I found the wind had increased to gale force as we made 8 knots, close hauled in rough seas. I reefed the main and staysail and bore away to avoid ships dead ahead and astern which seemed to be on my great circle course. I climbed on to the navigation seat and was about to pull down the padded arm to keep me in when I was forcibly ejected, wiping off the fire extinguisher and bracket en route to the galley where I landed so fast that I arrived before I knew I had started.

The BBC had instructed me on operating the video camera installed shortly before I left. The inside position was easy as the camera was clamped to the bulkhead with a view only of the chart table; but outside it had to be housed in a transparent waterproof container secured to the pushpit giving a view of the cockpit. It took some time to set up, what with its wires, remote control and microphone, so it was never available in rough weather or for emergencies when I was too hard pressed to stop and fix it up. Apparently the battery ran down if it was left on standby in advance. The battery was recharged from the ship's 12 volt batteries. Apart from the video I was lent a super 8 cine camera and given the film, and I bought myself a still camera. I took quite a lot of footage, but with no experience of filming, the results were not particularly dramatic.

The wind veered next day to north northeast force 6–7 on the starboard quarter. I handed the main and sailed first under genoa and staysail and then under genoa only as the staysail masked the big foresail. This gave me 7 knots and a steady platform after being thrown about the day before, but an unexpected wave crashed down the companionway so I hastily inserted the bottom transparent washboard. The vessel was more or less on an even keel and I was able to mop up and clear up, but the shallow bilges were full of water and the bilge pump suction hose was blocked. I looked around vainly for something with which to rod it through. When I mentioned this to John over the radiotelephone he suggested the Bosham burgee stick the Club had given me. This was a smart varnished job but it doubled wonderfully as a drain rod. There was much to do as I settled down to a routine of sail handling, deck work, navigation and battery charging.

I just managed to sail my planned track, set a bit to the north at the start. From 8 to 10 June the winds, mostly northeasterly, were up to 30 knots, giving a speedy sail but in poor visibility. The day's run on 10 June of 157 miles averaged just over 6½ knots; on that day I learned that eight yachts had already retired, mostly through breakages. I loved it out there. It was so interesting, and with ever changing situations there was so much to do. I felt quite at home. In the first week I had sailed 1000 miles, a third of the way. If the winds kept up and all went well, perhaps I could make the crossing in three weeks.

However, light winds came from ahead and either tack set me well off track in drizzle and poor visibility. We were becalmed all night and battered the next day by squalls of more than 30 knots of wind. The Autohelm 6000 could not hold her which was strange, since it had managed so far, in all conditions. To ease the helm I furled the genoa and found that the Autohelm was in fact broken, the driving rod attached to the quadrant having presumably sheered. As the electronic read-out was still operational, it had to be a mechanical breakdown again. Both the self-steering equipment and the cooker attachments had inherent faults needing redesign. What a time to fail.

I managed to rig the backup Autohelm 3000 in force 7 winds, which was quite difficult what with reefing and juggling with the helm. I locked the wheel until it was working. Four hours later the 3000 also ceased to function. I locked the wheel again. Having had no sleep for over twenty-four hours I was exhausted and catnapped for ten minutes at a time during the dark hours, dashing out to set *Flying Light* back on course when she veered off. I had breakfast at 0200 hours and started the generator for battery charging, ready to try remedies at dawn, hopefully with the wind dropping. Somehow the staysail leech line had caught inside the bearing out pole stowed up the mainmast and bar taut, had gathered up the leech of the sail. The pole had to be dismantled before the leech could be desnarled. This was slow work in rough weather. I was hooked on at all times to the jackstay or to secure points, once up the companionway.

Pressing on

It was now decision time. I had no self-steering, and it was 1,200 miles back to England, 500 miles to the Azores and at least 2,000 miles to America. I said out loud, 'What's going

138

on?' I had such a strong feeling I would make Newport. There was no way I was going back; I hate turning back at any time.

Although the Azores were comparatively close, the high pressure intensifying in that area could becalm me for days, and the lack of facilities there implied expense, delay and perhaps the loss of impetus to continue. I decided to press on to Newport, although I was not looking forward to the exhaustion of steering by hand and heaving to or furling sails to sleep. This would be even more difficult when passing over the Newfoundland Banks with fog, ice and fishing fleets, and when approaching land.

Next day was calm but just what I needed to get all the jobs done. I decided to check that the driving rod on the main autopilot had in fact sheered off the steering quadrant. This meant heaving out all the gear from the lazarette and temporarily stowing it elsewhere, unscrewing the deck boards and standing on my head while straining to examine the rod. The fitting on the end had broken, so that was that. Later that evening the diesel generator which charged the batteries failed. The fuel supply to that engine proved to be comprehensively self-airlocking, which it was beyond my capacity to cure. As the main engine consumed far more fuel than the generator, its use for battery charging would have to be restricted. I also lost use of the electric jug and kettle, which needed 240 volts AC, as the main alternator provided only 12 volts DC.

After discussions by radiotelephone with John and Malcolm I carried out tests on the failed backup autopilot to discover whether the 12 volt batteries were delivering power to the control box. Cheerfully, they were, so then I dismantled the electronic box of tricks to find that a lead had jumped out of its terminal. I righted this, and after two days of considerable difficulty I had self-steering again: absolute bliss.

Having eaten most of my fresh food except for cheese, eggs

and some fruit, I switched off the little refrigerator to save fuel for battery charging. I stopped using the weatherfax machine which printed weather forecasts on synoptic charts transmitted from Northwood, Bracknell and American and Canadian stations. With hindsight this was a mistake, but I was desperately anxious to economise on fuel. The radar put a heavy drain on the batteries so it would have to be reserved for restricted visibility and when I slept. I still had to report my position daily on the high frequency radiotelephone which consumed some 150 watts when transmitting.

Race rules obliged us to have non-mechanical means of generating power; John had installed solar panels and a wind generator providing sufficient charge to keep the autopilot going should the main engine alternator also fail. My economy routine was to charge the batteries evening and early morning. When they were topped up I could switch on the radar with its efficient alarm while I slept. Extremely vigilant about keeping a proper look out, I remained on the *qui vive* throughout the voyage notwithstanding the alarm system.

The genoa car control line shackle came apart but I managed to replace it by cannibalising a couple of shackles and a block. Becalmed again, the sails hung limply as the swell caused the wind vane on the mast top to rotate through 360°. Portuguese men-of-war sailed by, propelled by their inflated transparent bags, and dolphins, friendly and beautiful, practically invited themselves on board for lunch. Even the genoa sheets snarled up round the forestay and proved difficult to unravel. In the process I must, inadvertently, have unwound some line from the furling drum, which was to cause problems.

At last came twenty-four hours of force 4 increasing to 30 knots by late evening when we were making to windward in a nasty sea which was out of all proportion to the strength of the wind, due to a cross swell. I furled the genoa that night only to find, as I had feared, that I had run out of line on the drum before the sail was fully in, so I had to carry on with the remainder of the genoa set until the weather moderated. I was longing to sleep but had constantly to trim main and staysail. With the loss of the generator I could no longer recharge the batteries from below deck. It was necessary to go out to the after end of the cockpit repeatedly, first to start the main engine for charging and then to check and adjust the rpm as the engine warmed up. This was not very convenient in rough weather and darkness. I always stayed awake when the generator or the engine were in action and now that I was economising on fuel, I read books with a torch rather than use the cabin lights.

When the wind fell light I decided to lower the genoa in order to detach it from the foil and allow me to put more turns of the furling line on the drum. In strong winds the genoa furled in very tight rolls on the forestay, requiring extra line on the rotating drum. As the autopilot would not hold the vessel head to wind, there was little hope of lowering the sail on to the deck, and sure enough it went over the side. The sail was large and like a huge bucket filled with water. It took all my strength to haul it back on board. I detached the tack, the head of the sail and the swivel, lashed them and set about rolling on more turns, then hoisted and furled the sail. I was soaking wet and realised I had not eaten all day. Everything was much slower on one's own.

To economise, the radar was switched off during daylight hours in clear visibility, and I set my alarm clock pinger at fifteen minute intervals to remind me to look out for shipping. The wind rose to 30 knots and on furling the genoa, again I nearly ran out of line. This was rather nerve racking, because if the line pulled right out of the drum there was nothing to prevent the sail unfurling itself fully. In strong winds this might overpower the vessel, and I would have to get it down to the deck in quick time. Clearly I had failed to take into account the fact that the sail had been slackly furled in calm weather, when it appeared to have had more turns on the drum than were actually there.

I decided against lowering the sail, although the wind had decreased to 20 knots. When the genoa was furled I could not reach the clew to detach the sheets, so I brought them forward to pass round the forestay as I put more turns of the line on the drum. However, they became so entangled that I had to abandon this method. I unrove the 65 foot furling line from the leads to the cockpit winch and brought it forward, threaded the bitter end through the guard and round and round the drum, coiling the rope repeatedly to prevent it from falling overboard as I sat in the bows soaked with water, as the vessel dipped into the rough head sea. This time I made sure I had plenty of line on the drum and it was a success.

Fifteen days out I reckoned that I had fallen about four days behind the schedule I was hoping to sustain, struggling with a succession of minor equipment failures and with the intermittent calms. On calling up Portishead Radio to report my position one day, I was given a message from the yacht *Largo* (John Passmore), asking me to join in intership conversations with other singlehanded sailors at 1945 hours each evening. *Largo*, *British Heart* (James Hatfield) and *Freebird* (Peter Connole) and other competitors came and went in various languages, exchanging local weather information and discussing problems. The conversation was most interesting and cheerful. Trouble with furling genoas appeared to have beset several of us.

I had been having difficulty when using the radiotelephone. Every time I pressed the transmit pressel-switch to speak, the yacht went wildly off course, often with sails aback, so that my conversations were interrupted by my leaping on deck to retrieve the situation. Eventually I discovered that the compass for the backup autopilot contained within the control box in the cockpit, was too near the lead to the backstay which formed the high frequency aerial. The tremendous power generated when transmitting set up an electromagnetic field which sent the autopilot compass wild. To make a call meant either heaving to or handing the sails and disconnecting the autopilot. This was a serious waste of time and very frustrating because it could take up to two hours to get through when the air waves were exceptionally busy and my power insufficiently strong for me to be heard clearly. Portishead were always cheerful, professional and helpful even when temporarily I had to abandon my call, and they always made a special effort to connect with competitors when they heard the message 'yacht race report'.

The next few days were a mixture of very light and very strong winds of up to 35 knots, lumpy seas and poor visibility. By 25 June I heard that seventeen yachts had finished, three had struck whales or underwater wreckage and sunk, one had been abandoned and fourteen had retired. The winner was Phillippe Poupon in his 60 foot trimaran *Fleury Michon* in the incredible time of ten days, nine hours and fifteen minutes.

I was getting three hours sleep at a time until thick, miserable, soaking wet fog arrived from a depression passing through over two days, interspersed with squalls, torrential rain and a 30 knot wind quite unable to make up its mind from which direction it wanted to blow. I have never known such unremitting, soaking rain. I was endlessly reefing, shaking out reefs and trimming the sheets as the wind veered and backed. Once again I was on ten minute survival sleeping. For this no preparation was needed other than setting my alarms. I would lie down in the after cabin in wet oilskins and boots, fling an open sleeping bag over me and was gone in seconds, but was usually awake again before the alarm went off. The rain clouds tracking across the radar screen activated its warning system, making it useless for detecting ships. During a lull with all sails set I overslept for three hours through four backup alarms. I must have been exhausted. The noise of the sails brought me to the deck at 0200 hours to find it blowing hard at over 35 knots. Overpowered, I had a struggle to reef, and of course later in the day I was becalmed again. Would I ever make any progress? Never satisfied, I was now longing for strong winds again.

On Monday 27 June we entered the shallows of the Newfoundland Banks into soundings. The echo sounder was touching bottom after the ocean deeps. I had laid a track to pick up the cold Labrador current flowing in my direction adjacent to the warm contrary Gulf Stream. I did not want to be further north as the Banks were much wider there, and it would take longer to cross with many more days of poor visibility as the warm moist air passing over the cold current condensed to below its dew point causing fog. Once over the Banks, America seemed within reach although Newport was still 1000 miles away. It was very exciting.

At night while crossing the Newfoundland Banks thick fog suddenly closed in. I went below from my watch on deck to switch on the radar. A target appeared immediately on the screen so I started a radar plot and worked out it would pass 5 cables ahead of me. Back on deck I could barely see the bow. Suddenly I was startled by extremely noisy engines alongside *Flight* and men's voices shouting in panic. I could hear them clearly but could see nothing. Their powerful working lights were switched on but I could barely see them. I shone my bright Seabeam torch in their direction which brought an immediate response of more shouting. If they were fishing vessels it was my duty to keep clear of them, but I had no idea which way to turn as the noise encompassed me. I switched on the after deck and spreader lights and grabbed the engine keys and a pair of pliers in case I needed to break the seal and start the main engine for emergency manoeuvres.

My guess was that *Flight*'s radar reflector gave off a pretty good blip which may have led them to think I was a fair sized ship. Slowly the engine noises became fainter and I dashed below for a quick look at the radar to see several vessels emerging from the clutter at the screen's centre. That was why I had not seen their echo before. On reflection, I guessed the trawler fleet must have been at anchor and as I arrived on the scene had just started up their machinery for fish processing, which sounded so different from normal engine noise. Being at anchor would also have accounted for the fact that they were all around me for so long. In variable visibility the danger of using the radar only occasionally was evident. This gave me no chance to plot course, speed and closest point of approach of nearby vessels if they were hidden by the clutter at the centre of the radar screen when I first switched on.

The fuel storage for the generator was designed to allow me constant use of the radar, but the loss of the generator and the need to economise led me into this difficulty. I stayed up for the rest of the night with radar and deck lights switched on making great demands on the batteries. I dared not start the engine to charge them as I was listening for the sound of other vessels' engines as well as monitoring the radar screen. Later over the radiotelephone I heard that other competitors had also had alarming experiences with fishing vessels. It was very cold. Eventually a weak sun came out in the gloomy sky but did not lift the mist at deck level, and the sea was unusually disturbed with only 16 knots of southwesterly wind. I decided that I must have a nap.

18

Last Lap

By Tuesday 28 June I was just emerging from the Banks, out of soundings and into the ocean deeps again, hoping that the visibility would improve. The electronic satellite navigator stopped accepting satellite passes for position fixing. I had been using the sextant for checking the electronic aids, but now I was completely dependent on it. Also the sonic speed log indicated unbelievable speeds thus exaggerating distance covered. I streamed the backup Stowe log and reverted to basic navigation. Then large, confused cross seas developed with a southerly wind force 7 and rain clouds stalking across the radar screen. As night fell the 3000 autopilot failed again. I changed the drive belt before noticing that the screws and nuts clamping the small drive belt drum to the yacht's wheel had worked loose. Once tightened all was well again. Out there the forces on the gear were relentless.

The last few days I had been short of sleep and could have done with a good meal, but I was still cheerful and optimistic. The ungimballed stove was too time consuming and dangerous for cooking hot meals, and tinned food was not appetizing. I usually had a good breakfast any time between 0200 and 1000 hours in case I was so busy I forgot to eat for the rest of the day. This consisted of orange juice, two boiled eggs, crisp long-life French bread cooked in the oven, and coffee. I had many large bottles of soda water which was nicer than tank water to drink and also served to provide emergency liquid should the water tanks leak. The eggs became mouldy and started to taste odd. They should have been moved into the air once the refrigerator was switched off, but where could I have stowed them?

2 July was a lovely sailing day with a beam wind which after dark leapt to 45 knots, severe gale force 9. All sail was set at the time, so all hell let loose with tremendous squalls, heavy rain and huge seas. I leapt from my bunk, switched on the deck lights and battled to bring in the sails. Next day the weather then settled down to a pattern of calm night and morning and wind in the afternoon and evening, which meant only half the potential daily average in miles was logged. Extremely beautiful sunsets and bright moonlit nights were followed by stunning dawns.

I was steering well to the south of the dangerous low lying Sable Island in longitude 60°W, Zone +4. I kept GMT on all the clocks and watches, which meant the sunsets and dawns were later and later each day. I began to think I would never reach Newport, and as I listened over the air others felt the same. Estimated times of arrival went astray as we were becalmed again while friends, relations and owners turned up in Newport.

I was headed and driven north of my track on port tack as starboard tack would have taken me southwards into the contrary Gulf Stream. The Loran chain which is available from American stations came in giving a direct read out of latitude and longitude. I really was warming to these electronic aids. Large ships passed. Radar plots of relative velocity triangles to find out their closest point of approach, when and how far they would pass ahead or astern of me or whether they would hit me became academic, as I was totally becalmed and could not move out of their way! Over the radiotelephone on Tuesday 5 July I heard that *British Heart* had arrived in Newport, and suddenly John and Geraldine were on board her and talking to me. Hugh and his friend Jane Bilton were on their way via Boston. I couldn't wait to get in.

On 6 July, approaching Odas buoy some 300 miles from Newport, pilot whales played around me and later I saw a gigantic black V-shaped tail of a whale disappearing beneath the surface just ahead of me. I kept a wary eye out as I had heard over the radio that one competitor had sunk after colliding with a whale, had taken to his liferaft and was rescued by a ship after sending out a distress call. Another competitor, Mike Birch in his 60 foot trimaran *Fujicolor*, had also hit a whale and flooded his main hull. After sending out a distress call he decided to stay with the yacht and sailed her back to France in eleven days, the last three without food.

I was up all night dodging fishing vessels and unlit fishing buoys with reflectors which showed up on radar only when close to. Later, to get more sleep, I trained myself to discriminate between continuous radar alarms indicating other vessels, and short bleeps, the characteristic of little buoys in a seaway. Although I was woken up by the small bleeps, I disregarded them. By day I could see stationary trawlers to starboard, processing their fish. Some would start to move and always, it seemed, in my direction passing close, presumably following the fish. 'Oh, for some wind.' I was forced to alter course to the south to clear the trawlers, but wanted to avoid being set into the Nantucket traffic separation scheme.

On 8 July I passed south of the Nantucket shoals in thick fog, hoping soon to bear away for the last 75 miles to the finishing line at Brenton Reef Tower. Now there was more wind and traffic but less visibility. I had not eaten or slept properly all day with so much shipping to plot, but by evening the mist and the traffic had cleared and I had a much needed sleep, having only catnapped over the last twenty-four hours. During that time the autopilot went considerably off course with the change of wind direction, and the genoa snarled. I spent quite some time that night struggling to free it.

The Loran kept telling me that I was being pushed north. I had entered the area of tidal streams. The diamonds on the chart confirmed the stream was north going, for which I had already compensated, but this seemed excessive. Finally the Loran put me right in the middle of a shoal and I said out loud, 'don't be ridiculous, I'm not there.' It went on climbing to higher and higher latitudes. Much later on I learned it was not my receiver but the Loran transmitting station itself which had failed.

I had been well off course while I slept, the sonic speed log remained unserviceable and condensation behind the glass made the electronic towed log unreadable. I updated two estimated positions on the chart from my last known position: the first assumed that the self-steering had been accurate; the second was my guess at the possible off-track error. Both positions were uncertain due to the lack of accurate log distance. I kept the two plots going simultaneously from then on, while I waited for dawn to get star sights and later on sun sights, but as the sky lightened the visibility closed in again. Still uncertain of my position, I turned on to a northwesterly course for the last leg towards the finishing line. I sailed all day in poor visibility. The coastline was not distinctive on radar and I was unable to pick up any radio beacons. Brenton Reef Tower was apparently difficult to find at the best of times. As I closed the shore I reckoned I was to the east of it, so turned on to a westerly heading, and there it was dead ahead through the haze on long spindly legs. I called up the Royal Western Yacht Club officials who were at Newport and crossed the line at 2100 GMT, 1700 hours Newport summer time on Saturday 9 July.

At last the tow boat arrived with family and friends on board, shouting and waving with excitement. Brenton Reef Tower is about two miles outside Newport harbour and I was taken in tow as I reached the entrance to the Narrows. They berthed me and everyone came aboard. There were hugs, champagne and a great cheer from fellow competitors, some of whom I had been talking to over the radiotelephone and whose voices now had faces. John, his sister Jan, Hugh, Geraldine and their friends were beside themselves with excitement. My tired brain and body switched off and I just enjoyed the fuss. I had hardly eaten or slept over the last thirty-six hours but who cared, I was in. I had logged 3,600 nautical miles in thirty-four days and ten hours to finish seventy-first. Of the ninety-five starters, a quarter failed to finish. Seventeen yachts were forced to retire, three sank and two were abandoned, including little *Jester*, a veteran of every race since the first in 1960.

Epilogue

Geraldine, John and his sister Jan had to return to England the day after I had arrived in Newport. Jan Reid, a Fleet Street journalist, had given me invaluable help with the press. Their rapid departure was disappointing for me, but they had already been in Newport a week, having got there too early, and had to return to their work. Hugh and Jane had planned to stay on and see something of America. In the event both remained in Newport and unstintingly gave of their time and energy as I was exhausted and needed help with the repairs to *Flight*.

Hugh took up the strain. He did the detailed design work and organisation of a clever repair to the mechanical part of the main autopilot. Hood's kindly made this up in their workshop to his specifications. He spent much time in trying to get assistance with the electronics and generator repairs before John returned, but had considerable difficulty, as the main yacht yard was on strike and it was the height of the Newport season. He had no success with the generator. I had a lot of help in Newport from very many people and much local press and television coverage. John returned to join me for the two-handed voyage back to England and worked very hard to get the vessel ready for sea. He found some excellent help from Autohelm after an electronic fault developed and from an engineer who refashioned the rubber mountings for the generator which fuel leaks had dissolved.

We slipped Newport Yachting Centre on 28 July and steered due east for the first week, keeping to the warm favourable Gulf Stream in roughly latitude 40°N, far to the south of the fog, fishing vessels and contrary current of the Newfoundland Banks. We were working our way along the northern fringe of the Bermuda/Azores high pressure zone with blue skies, sunny weather, calm nights, full moon, bright stars and mostly following breezes. Flying fish landed on the deck. We rigged twin whisker poles for the headsails and also the big light weather reaching genoa set flying on the spinnaker halliard.

We were accompanied nearly all the way by two storm petrels. They maintained open escort during the day and close escort during the night. They twittered to each other through the darkness as they kept station with us; little scraps of birds, their only home at sea on the wing, a life permanently buffeted by the Atlantic wastes. We passed through a large school of pilot whales steering a reciprocal course. They were in line abreast and stretched about two cables on each side of us as we passed nervously through the middle of the line.

To the north of us the Atlantic lows were now powering their way eastwards in an endless succession. We were a week out, and the winds had increased to west northwest force 7–8. We ran under reefed main and staysail with quartering seas building up rapidly and a cross swell. With washboards in, we were flying along before the ferocious following sea under blue skies and large cumulus clouds. A few hours before we planned to swing northwards at about longitude 50°W on to a great circle course for the Scillies, tropical revolving storm 'Albert' appeared on the weatherfax synoptic chart, tracking

154

up the Canadian shore. We decided to press on eastwards for another thirty-six hours, which moved us out of harm's way.

About 350 miles north of the Azores, a large, bright blue fishing vessel bore down on us fast from dead astern. It was rather alarming. She then proceeded to circle us with much enthusiastic waving from all the crew who had lined the deck seemingly intrigued by a yacht so far out. Off they went to fish, returning later, when I called them up on VHF. When they asked if I spoke Spanish my answer was negative, so they went back to their work.

We had slid past the Azores sufficiently far north to avoid the worst of the calms and now entered the southern fringes of the low pressure systems in which we remained until we reached soundings in the western approaches. A small school of whales joined us and for two hours played follow my leader with us. At times we had a fifteen footer within a whisker of our rudder. Two young ones were chasing each other down the face of the steep seas immediately behind our stern. John went below for a cup of tea!

The power of most of these low pressure systems was considerable and they unremittingly drove us homeward with strong following winds and big following seas. One of these systems gave us a four day bashing with wind speeds up to force 9 and very fierce cross seas. We were thrown about the vessel from the yawing, pitching and rolling on this turbulent ride. With only a reefed staysail set, we ran at 6–7 knots surfing at 10 knots with a most uncomfortable corkscrew motion. Throughout the twenty-eight day voyage the autopilot steered the vessel continuously. Not once did we lay a hand on the wheel and we never had the wind forward of the beam at any time. John spent the calm days early in the voyage struggling with the generator, bleeding the fuel system and trying to make it work properly, all to no avail.

On 22 August we entered soundings. The transition was

striking: the seas on the continental shelf were completely different in character from those experienced in the deep. The waves were now smaller and steeper, the cross seas less evident. Up the English Channel it was wet, cold, windy and miserable. The shipping traffic became heavier as we made our way towards the Solent. Geraldine, an excellent communications' coordinator for both voyages, was very cagey over the radiotelephone about her arrangements and on the day before we arrived insisted that we entered Portsmouth harbour at 1030 hours exactly. At 2300 hours on 24 August we rounded Anvil Point and reached the shelter of Poole Bay. With the weather still wet and windy, force 7, we would be too early for the tidal stream in the Needles Channel, so blew some of the way there under bare poles. The night was dark and visibility poor from the rain. Somehow the charts of the area had been inadvertently sent ashore at Plymouth before the start of the Race. John was most put out and said we were in danger of wrecking ourselves on the last lap. He retired to his berth muttering, 'filthy black night and no maps!' I set to work hastily. Using a plotting sheet with latitude scale and inserting longitude and data from the almanacs, I made a chart of the Needles Channel and approaches showing the positions and characteristics of all the lights and buoys – situation retrieved!

Once in the Solent we were too early for our rendezvous at Portsmouth. The tidal stream was favourable and *Flight* refused to slow down even with no sails set. It was 25 August and I was tired of hanging about and wanted to get into port. In the event we were a few minutes late arriving at Campers marina, having been delayed by a mad rush of departing yachts and ferries converging at Portsmouth harbour entrance.

We were met with the most incredible welcome. Friends and supporters, the press and local TV had all turned up and were lining the dockside to greet us with hooters, cheers, 'welcome home' banners and champagne. The lines went ashore. Friends swarmed aboard.

Glossary

Abeam: at right angles to the vessel's fore and aft line.

Amidships: half way between bow and stern.

Back: wind changing direction anticlockwise.

Backstay: a wire rigged from masthead to stern to support the mast.

Bar taut: rope stretched rigid under great tension.

Beam sea: a rolling sea at right angles to the fore and aft line of the vessel.

Bearing out pole: a pole set to hold out the sail when running before the wind.

Beat to windward: a yacht cannot sail head to wind so must tack close either side of the wind in a series of zigzag courses.

Beaufort wind scale: see page 165.

Bilge: the rounded part of the hull bottom, inside which, water collects.

Bitter end: the inboard end of a mooring rope or anchor cable when made fast to the vessel.

Block: can be used to lead a rope in any direction. Also used as a pulley.

Boom: a spar or pole at right angles to the mast on which to set a sail.

Bulkhead: a rigid cross partition in a ship.

Cable: is one tenth of a nautical mile, 608 feet, roughly 200 yards.

Chart datum: is the level of lowest astronomical tide under average meteorological conditions. It is the level above which drying heights, and below which soundings are given on the chart. It is also the level above which heights of tides are given in the tables.

Cleat: wood or metal fitting with horns used for securing ropes or moorings on deck.

Clew: the after corner of the sail.

Clinker: boat construction where each timber plank overlaps the one below it.

Close hauled: sailing as close to the wind as possible.

Companionway: vessel's ladder or staircase to below decks.

Cruising chute: a very large light weather balloon shaped sail.

Cuddy: a hard top over the forward part of the boat, open aft.

Cutter: a sailing vessel with one mast, a mainsail and two foresails.

Deadlights: strong covers fitted to ports to protect them in storm conditions.

Direction finding (DF): an instrument capable of obtaining bearings from radio beacons.

Dodger: canvas screen.

Double headed yawl: a two masted yacht with two foresails.

Drogue or sea anchor: streamed over the stern to act as a brake and to hold the yacht stern to the wind and waves when running. When streamed at the bow, to hold her head to wind.

160

Echo sounder: an instrument fitted inboard the vessel which is able to measure the depth of water by sound impulses.

Fairleads: fittings through which ropes are led to change direction of the lead without undue friction.
Fair tide: tidal stream flowing in the direction you are going.
Fathom: is six feet.
Fiddles: wooden frames or rails to prevent objects falling off tables or shelves when the vessel rolls or pitches.
Fin keel: an iron keel in the shape of a fin bolted to the underside of a yacht's hull.
Forestay: wire rigged from mast to bow to support the mast and to which the foresails are secured.
Freeboard: the height of the side of a vessel above the waterline.
Furling: stowing a sail.

Gaff rigged: a vessel whose mainsail is carried aloft by a combination of the mast and a spar called the gaff which extends the mast upwards and aft to the top of the sail.
Genoa: a large foresail.
Gimbal: a fitting which allows, say, a compass or a stove to remain horizontal when the yacht rolls.
Gybe: to turn a sailing vessel when the wind is aft so that the wind and the boom pass from one stern quarter to the other. (Opposite of tack.)

Halyards: ropes or wires used to hoist and lower sails.
Hand: to lower or furl, as of a sail, or to haul in.
Headed: desired course straight into the wind.
Heads: ship's lavatories.
Heave to: trim the sails by backing the foresail to take the way off the vessel for a rest or in heavy weather.
Helm: the yacht's tiller or wheel for steering.

Jackstay or lifeline: a wire or rope to which a safety harness line can be clipped to allow the crew safe movement round the deck.

Jury rig: a makeshift rig should the mast break.

Ketch: a two masted sailing vessel with the mizzenmast stepped before the rudder post.

Knockdown: Sailing boat laid over by wind or wave until her mast is horizontal.

Knot: one nautical mile per hour.

Lazy sheet: one of two foresail control ropes not in use at the time.

Leading lights or marks, or transits: set up in line to lead a vessel along safe water clear of dangers.

Lead line: a lead weight attached to a line marked in fathoms or metres which is swung over the vessel's side to measure depth of water.

Leech line: a line running down the trailing edge of the sail used to adjust the curve.

Lee shore: the shore which is down wind of the yacht and on which the vessel will be blown if she cannot make headway against the wind.

Leeway: the amount a vessel is blown down wind of her course.

Let go: release or cast off.

Lie a hull or bare poles: a sailing vessel with no sails set.

Log book: Ship's log where all information is recorded including courses steered, log distances, tidal information, weather etc.

Log: instrument with a rotator either fitted to the hull below the waterline or towed astern on a cable and used to measure distance travelled through the water.

Log line: the line of a log towed over the stern to which is attached a rotator.

Loran: an instrument capable of indicating the vessel's position using special shorebased radio transmissions.

Low: in meterology, a low pressure system giving bad weather.

Main sheet: the rope by which a mainsail is controlled and trimmed when sailing.

Mizzenmast: the after shorter mast on a two masted vessel.

Mizzen: a sail hoisted on the mizzen mast.

Nautical mile: is 6080 feet, roughly 2000 yards. Note: all miles when referred to at sea, are nautical miles.

Offing: distance from the shore.

Overfalls: waves that break violently over shoals or uneven sea bed and at the meeting of conflicting currents or in wind against tide conditions.

Peak: the upper corner of the sail.

Pilot berth: berth which is positioned outboard and above the side seats in the yacht's saloon.

Ports: portholes or windows.

Pushpit: a metal guardrail set up round the after deck (pulpit at the bow).

Reef: shorten sail.

Reaching: sailing with the wind at right angles to the boat.

Sampson post: a strong post through deck bolted, to which can be secured mooring ropes or towline.

Shackle: a metal link, U shaped with a removable pin used to close the mouth of the U. Also, fifteen fathoms of anchor cable is called a shackle.

Sheets: ropes attached to the clew of a sail used to control and trim it.

Shrouds: wires rigged from masthead to yacht's side to support the mast.

Sloop: single masted yacht with mainsail and foresail.

Soundings: the depth of the sea bed below chart datum level. Also means water of a depth shallow enough to be measured by lead line or conventional sounding equipment.

Spade rudder: a rudder which is hung beneath the hull from the rudder post within the hull. It is in the form of a fin without any support at its leading edge.

Springs: spring tides are the highest and the lowest tides and the fastest tidal streams.

Staysail: inner foresail.

Storm sail or jib: a very small foresail for use in heavy weather.

Tack: to turn the bow of the vessel through the wind on to port or starboard tack (opposite to gybe).

Tackle: a purchase formed by use of rope and blocks to lighten a load.

Tiller: a wood or metal bar for steering the boat.

Transit: see leading marks.

Triatic stay: a horizontal stay or wire between the tops of two masts.

Trick: trick at the wheel or helm, time spent steering.

Trysail: a very small storm sail set instead of the mainsail in heavy weather.

Unrove, unreeve: to draw a rope out from a block or lead.

Veer: wind changing direction clockwise. Also to pay out anchor cable.

Washboards: boards inserted vertically in opening to the cabin to close the gap between hatch and deck.

Way: the movement of the vessel through the water.

Weather shore: the wind blowing off the shore, blowing the yacht away from danger.

Weigh anchor: raise the anchor from the sea bed.

Whisker pole: a light weather pole used to boom out fore-sails when running before the wind.

Yawl: a two masted sailing vessel with the mizzenmast stepped aft of the rudder post.

Beaufort Scale of Wind Force

Beaufort Number	Wind speed in knots	General description
0	0	calm
1	1–3	light air
2	4–6	light breeze
3	7–10	gentle breeze
4	11–16	moderate breeze
5	17–21	fresh breeze
6	22–27	strong breeze
7	28–33	near gale
8	34–40	gale
9	41–47	severe gale
10	48–55	storm
11	56–63	violent storm
12	64 and over	hurricane

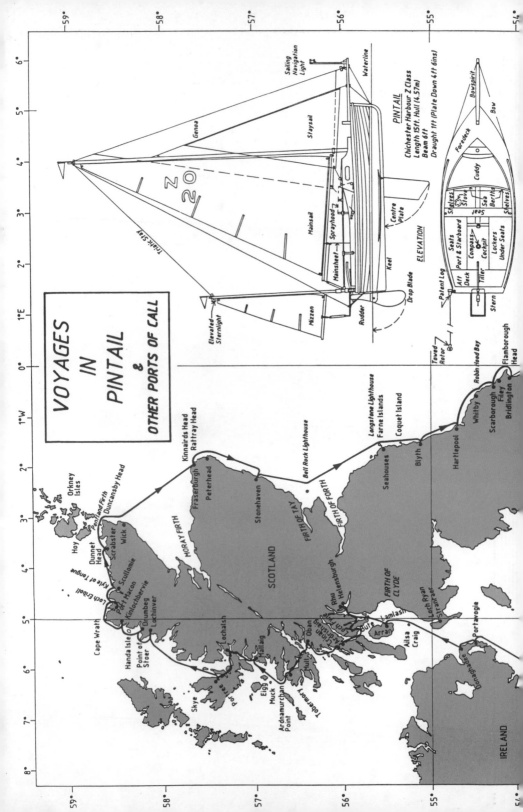

VOYAGES
IN
PINTAIL
&
OTHER PORTS OF CALL

PINTAIL

Chichester Harbour Z Class
Length 15ft. Hull (4.57m)
Beam 6ft
Draught 1ft (Plate Down 4ft 6ins)

ELEVATION

Sailing Navigation Light
Waterline
Genoa
Staysail
Mainsail
Spraysheet
Mainsail
Mainsheet
Mizzen
Rudder
Elevated Sternlight
Drop Blade
Keel
Centre Plate
Traffic Stay
Z 20

Towed Rotor
B

Bowsprit
Bow
Foredeck
Cuddy
Shelves
Stove
Seats
Port & Starboard
Compass
Cockpit
Sea
Berths
Shelves
1805
Lockers
Under Seats
Aft
Deck
Tiller
Stern
Patent Log

Orkney Isles
Hoy
Dunnet Head
Scrabster
Wick
Scullomie
Kyle of Tongue
Port Macon
Kinlochbervie
Drumbeg
Lochinver
Cape Wrath
Handa Isle
Point of Stoer
Loch Erboll
Penland Firth
Duncansby Head
MORAY FIRTH
Kinnairds Head
Rattray Head
Fraserburgh
Peterhead
Stonehaven
FIRTH OF TAY
FIRTH OF FORTH
Bell Rock Lighthouse
Longstone Lighthouse
Farne Islands
Coquet Island
Seahouses
Blyth
Hartlepool
Robin Hood Bay
Whitby
Scarborough
Filey
Bridlington
Flamborough Head

SCOTLAND

Lochalsh
Mallaig
Skye
Portree
Eigg
Muck
Ardnamurchan Point
Tobermory
Mull
Oban
Loch Crinan
Crinan
Kerrera
Gigha
Rhu
Helensburgh
FIRTH OF CLYDE
Bute
Arran
Ailsa Craig
Lamlash
Loch Ryan
Stranraer
Portavogie
Donaghadee

IRELAND